best ever

 low fat

p

This is a Parragon Publishing Book
First published in 2003

Parragon Publishing
Queen Street House
4 Queen Street
Bath BA1 1HE
United Kingdom

Created and produced by
The Bridgewater Book Company Ltd,
Lewes, East Sussex

Photographer Ian Parsons

ISBN: 1–40541–688–2

Printed in China

NOTE

This book uses imperial, metric, or US cup measurements. Follow the same
units of measurement throughout; do not mix imperial and metric. All spoon
measurements are level: teaspoons are assumed to be 5 ml and tablespoons are
assumed to be 15 ml. Unless otherwise stated, milk is assumed to be whole,
eggs, and individual vegetables such as potatoes are medium, and pepper is
freshly ground black pepper.

The times given for each recipe are an approximate guide only.
The preparation times may differ according to the techniques used by different
people and the cooking times may vary as a result of the type of oven used.
Ovens should be preheated to the specified temperature. If using a fan-assisted
oven, check the manufacturer's instructions for adjusting the time and temperature.
The preparation times include chilling and marinating times, where appropriate.

The nutritional information provided for each recipe is per serving or per
portion. Optional ingredients, variations, or serving suggestions have not been
included in the calculations.

Recipes using raw or very lightly cooked eggs should be avoided
by infants, the elderly, pregnant women, convalescents, and anyone
suffering from an illness.

contents

introduction

As we are becoming more aware of how we can improve our own and our families' health, lowfat cooking is becoming increasingly popular. However, lowfat food is often wrongly perceived as being "diet" food and, therefore, boring, bland, and unappetizing. This is simply not true and this book will help to change any misconceptions. Lowfat cooking is healthier and often less expensive, and there is a huge variety of tasty dishes.

From day-to-day family suppers to sophisticated dinner parties, this book is packed with delicious recipe ideas and tips. You will find many family favorites in the following pages, such as Easy Gazpacho (see page 22), Pasta with Lowfat Pesto (see page 58), Meatballs with Tomato Relish (see page 116), and Smoked Haddock Pie (see page 176). There is even a selection of lowfat sandwich fillings for quick and easy snacks.

While nutritionists and health professionals agree that most people in the Western world eat too much fat, this does not mean that you should try to cut it out of your diet completely. Everybody needs to consume a certain amount of fat for general health and well-being. Fats are a concentrated source of energy and provide valuable vitamins. Essential fats are—as their name suggests—essential. The type of fat consumed is as important as the quantity (see page 6). However, as a rule, your daily intake of fats should not exceed more than 30 percent of the day's total average of 2,000 calories (for adults). As each gram of fat provides nine calories, simple arithmetic shows that the average daily intake of fat should be no more than 2½ oz (66.7 g).

Some people can eat nothing but burgers and fries and still stay slim, but this does not mean that they are healthy. By doing more exercise and having a higher metabolic rate, you can burn off more of the fat you have consumed, but you will not be as healthy as your friend who consumes less fat and exercises moderately. Whether you want to lose weight, have been told to eat less fat by your doctor or simply want to improve your family's health, use this book to guide you to a healthier and happier lifestyle. This book also includes tips on how to choose lower-fat ingredients in place of the butter, cream, cheese, and red meats to which we have all become accustomed, as well as advice on healthy cooking techniques and useful equipment.

changing your eating patterns

Food is always more appetizing if it is presented attractively. All of the recipes in this book use color and style, as well as flavor and texture, to make your meal thoroughly enjoyable. If you are entertaining guests, why not try one of the following combinations? For vegetarian guests, serve Lentil & Tomato Soup (see page 25), followed by Roast Summer Vegetables (see page 72), and Lemon Granita (see page 229). Serve Prosciutto with Figs (see page 49), Beef in Beer (see page 117), and Hot Chocolate Cherries (see page 220) as a winter meal for meat-lovers. Chicken & Asparagus Timbales (see page 44), followed by Lamb Tagine (see page 134), and Peach Sherbet (see page 230), is an ideal meal for a party.

The recipes featured in this book are just a few of the many delicious lowfat meals you can make. They vary in difficulty from quick and easy to more time-consuming and skillful. Many of the dishes are also suitable for freezing and reheating in an oven or microwave. You can even take them to work and heat them up at lunchtime, leaving no excuses for indulging in take-outs.

types of fat

Keeping track of which fats to eat and which to avoid, counting calories and keeping a wary eye on sugar and salt content can all seem overwhelming. The thing to remember is that too many saturated fats are harmful, but unsaturated fats in moderation are beneficial.

You will find saturated fats in foods such as red meat, butter, hard cheese (like Cheddar), cookies, cakes, pastries, and chocolate. Although they are mostly found in animal products, there are some vegetable sources too. Coconut and palm oil are both high in saturated fats, as are most fats that are solid at room temperature.

There are two different types of unsaturated fats—monounsaturated and polyunsaturated. Monounsaturated fats are better for you than saturated fats, but are not so good as polyunsaturated fats. Monounsaturated fats are found in olive oil, rapeseed oil, nuts, seeds, oily fish, and avocados. These are fine if consumed in moderate quantities and are thought to reduce cholesterol level in the blood. This may explain why there is a low incidence of heart disease in some Mediterranean countries where olive oil, avocados, and oily fish are eaten regularly.

The body needs polyunsaturated fats for various functions. Both omega-3 and omega-6 fatty acids are classed by nutritionists as essential. Omega-3 fatty acids are needed for healthy cells and brain development. Polyunsaturated fats help to protect against heart disease, arthritis, and some other medical conditions. Polyunsaturated fats are found in fish oils, oily fish, walnuts, olive oil, and sunflower-seed oil. They are usually liquid at room temperature.

Be careful of processed oils labeled "hydrogenated vegetable oils," as some of the good unsaturated fats are converted to unhealthy saturated fats—or trans fats—by the process used to make them.

cholesterol

Raised cholesterol levels in the blood are regarded as a cause for concern, as levels that are constantly high or rising are thought to cause heart disease. The best way to avoid this happening is to eat a varied and balanced diet. Cut out, or at least cut down on, foods such as solid cooking fats (shortening and hard margarine), cookies, cakes, chocolate, fatty meat, processed foods, and whole dairy products (butter, cream, and hard cheeses).

Medical research shows that if you cut down to almost no saturated fats, you may be able to reduce your blood cholesterol level by more than 10 percent. Foods thought to be helpful in reducing blood cholesterol levels include whole-grain bread, Granary bread, cereal containing cooked bran, rolled oats, oranges, apples, bananas, figs, prunes, garlic, onions, red kidney beans, and other beans. Try having Fruity Oat Crunch Bars (see page 253) as a low-cholesterol alternative to cakes.

a balanced diet

There are five main food groups, and you should try to eat a certain amount from each group daily. The first group consists of fruit and vegetables (not potatoes), and provides you mainly with vitamins and minerals. The advice is to eat at least five portions from this group per day and that at least some of them should be uncooked. This may sound like a lot, but you will be able to eat the daily recommendation if you spread it throughout the day—for example, choose a banana and cereal for breakfast, a sandwich with salad for lunch, and steamed chicken with broccoli, carrots, and peas for dinner. Try to snack on healthy alternatives to crisps and chocolate, such as fruit.

The second group includes staples such as rice, pasta, bread, potatoes, and cereals. These contain complex carbohydrates, which release energy at a steady rate, and dietary fiber, which aids digestion. It is recommended that we try to consume several servings of these foods each day. Having a rice salad (with a lowfat dressing) for lunch, potatoes with dinner, and Fat-free Marble Cake (see page 248) for dessert will be an adequate intake for most people. This group helps to keep your digestive system working efficiently and is thought to help lower the chances of stomach and bowel cancers.

The third food group is the protein foods—meat, fish, and poultry. Red meat can be high in saturated fats and you need to trim off any visible fat before cooking. Poultry and fish are the healthiest ingredients. Eat plenty of oily fish, such as sardines, mackerel, tuna, salmon, and herrings, as they are rich in omega-3 essential fatty acids. You do not need to eat foods from this group every day if you have a mixed diet. When you do eat them, you need only small quantities. About 25 percent of the fat we consume comes from meat and meat products. Even trimmed meats, such as lamb chops, pork loin, and fillet steak, can contain high amounts of fats. Vegetarians can sometimes have an inadequate intake of protein. They should take care to eat a varied diet that includes tofu and other vegetable proteins.

The fourth food group is made up of dairy products, including milk, cheese, and cream. You need a moderate amount of these foods daily. Growing children, pregnant women, and the elderly, especially those suffering from a bone disease such as osteoporosis, require a higher intake of calcium and should adjust their diets accordingly. Most dairy products contain a very high proportion of fats, and eating large amounts can make it more difficult to lose weight or keep blood cholesterol levels down. About 20 percent of the fat we consume comes from this food group.

Be careful about the fifth food group. It consists of foods that contain fat and sugar, such as margarine, chocolate, and sweet pastries. You need only very small amounts of food from this group as you will obtain the small intake of fat you require from other food groups.

Being aware of hidden fats is important. It is easy to cut down on fatty foods, but knowing where to look for the real lowfat alternatives is essential. Many nuts and seeds are rich in essential fatty acids, but also have quite a high overall fat content. Even trimmed "lean" meat can contain up to 10 percent fat.

A varied diet is a healthy diet, and you should aim to eat different foods each day, as they all have different combinations and quantities of nutrients. Try different types of pasta, such as Fettuccine with Smoked Salmon (see page 60) and Rigatoni with Squid (see page 204). When cooking pasta, resist the temptation to add a few drops of oil to the pan to prevent it sticking, as this raises the fat content. Making use of exotic fruits and vegetables will also make a lowfat diet more interesting.

lowfat cooking techniques

You may be used to putting a tablespoon of butter or shortening into the skillet before adding the lean bacon—this doesn't mean that you should. Instead of adding the saturated fat, try broiling without any added fat. Instead of lean, try extra lean bacon and trim off any fat. You could even get rid of the bacon altogether. Knowing what the alternatives are is the key to enjoying your new lowfat diet. You don't have to forego everything you enjoy eating. Sitting down to a family meal together can be one of the most pleasurable parts of your day.

It is worthwhile investing in good-quality, nonstick cookware. Cast iron, stainless steel, and heavy-gauge aluminum are ideal and you will find that you need very little fat, as the heat is evenly distributed. If you need to add fat, use oils high in unsaturated fats, such as olive or sunflower-seed oil. Cans of "spray oils" are even more effective at minimizing the amount you use, as you can give the pan a light, even coat.

As a rule, avoid frying, as it is the least healthy way of cooking. Stir-frying is better as long as you use very little oil. Use a good-quality wok and keep the temperature high, tossing the ingredients constantly so that they do not stick. Try Shrimp Stir-Fry (see page 206). The best advice about deep-frying is: don't!

Vegetables can be cooked in many ways and are often especially healthy when eaten raw. Try cooking them in juice, stock and/or wine for a tasty alternative to oil. Steamed vegetables have a more vibrant color, firmer texture, and retain more nutrients than boiled vegetables. Boiling vegetables is a no-fat way of cooking, but it also destroys many of their nutrients, especially vitamins. Try microwaving as a quick alternative to boiling or steaming.

Broiling and grilling are one of the healthiest methods of cooking and a number of foods can be cooked this way. Thread diced chicken and vegetables onto skewers, then grill or broil as kabobs. Grilling imparts a beautiful flavor to the food and is healthy, although be careful to eat vegetables to balance the protein. Try not to burn grilled food, as this is not only unappetizing, but is also believed to be carcinogenic (cancer-causing).

Griddling in a ridged grill pan is a healthy compromise between pan-frying and broiling. The food cooks rapidly and if oil is needed, lightly brushing over the griddle pan is all that is required. If poached chicken seems like boiled meat to you, try poaching chicken breasts in stock with white wine and herbs. You do not need to use any oil and you can steam vegetables over the pan while the meat is cooking. Poaching is also ideal for fish.

Instead of adding flavorings as you cook, you can use a marinade. Meat and poultry are made tender by marinating overnight or for at least 4 hours in a mixture of lemon juice, oil, herbs, garlic, and either vinegar or alcohol. Do not marinate fish for longer than 1 hour. When you are baking desserts, use good-quality bakeware. Use waxed paper or parchment paper to eliminate the need to coat the cake pans in butter before adding the mixture. A light brushing of oil is enough.

from high fat to low fat

When buying meat, ask your butcher to trim off any visible fat or to remove the bone so that you can easily trim the meat. If you shop in a supermarket, it is not easy to see what you are buying if it is prepacked. Buy from the delicatessen or butcher and do not be afraid to ask him to put a piece back and get you another.

Many supermarkets now stock a wide range of lowfat and low-calorie products, such as milk, cheese, yogurt, salad dressings, potato chips, and cookies. However, even if the label says "low fat," it is still best to have a look at the ingredients list. Avoid products labeled "reduced fat," as they may have a very high saturated fat content.

Lowfat spreads are available in every store and supermarket and it can be confusing to read all the labels, which make various claims. Generally, some are only for spreading and others are only for cooking. Olive oil provides the best flavor when cooking, but can be expensive to use regularly. For spreading, you can buy the very lowfat spreads, but these have a high water content and are not suitable for cooking. Spreads labeled low fat or half fat are suitable for spreading and baking and have a fat content of about 40 percent, compared with the very lowfat spreads with about 20 percent.

Gradually changing and enhancing your diet is far better and safer than suddenly stopping eating one thing and switching to another. There are many ways to re-adjust your diet and that of your family without extra financial cost or effort in the kitchen.

To start with, eat less of the foods that contain lots of saturated fats. Buy lowfat spreads and olive oil or polyunsaturated oils for cooking.

Limit fatty meats, such as lamb and pork, to occasional treats and eat chicken, turkey, fish, and venison instead. Trim any fat from the meat and remove the skin. If you are fond of a roast dinner, try putting a chicken on a rack with a roasting pan underneath. Cover it with herbs and garlic and baste occasionally with stock—cook at the same temperature and for the same length of time as a normal roast. Instead of making gravy the traditional way, try reducing stock or vegetable cooking water and freezing it in meal-size portions, then thicken with cornstarch and add salt, pepper, and herbs.

Instead of basing meals round meat, try a meal based round eggs, such as Mexican Eggs (see page 74), or round vegetables, such as Layered Vegetable Bake (see page 88). Sausages can be high in saturated fats—choose lowfat varieties or make your own. Prick them with a fork so that the fat can run out, place on a rack and broil.

Even if you are not a vegetarian, use tofu in place of meat sometimes for a healthy, lowfat alternative. Try Vegetable & Tofu Stir-Fry (see page 152).

Whole dairy products can raise blood cholesterol levels and contribute to obesity. This is a high risk for vegetarians, who often rely too heavily on cheese for protein. Avoid these whole products altogether and switch to lowfat or skim milk products, which will make a huge difference to your fat intake. lowfat yogurts are readily available in almost all grocery stores and are a great idea for a healthy lunch. Buy lowfat plain yogurt and use it as a substitute for cream to thicken sauces and add to desserts. A bowl of lowfat plain yogurt with honey or jelly (which contain no fat at all) makes a healthy and delicious start to the day. lowfat and fat free mascarpone cheese are also healthy options which can be used in both sweet and savory dishes.

Instead of buying French fries and potato chips, look for lowfat savory crackers and breadsticks. If you cannot find any, you can make your own by baking thin slices of potato coated with herbs and spices. Most supermarkets now have a range of very lowfat potato chips, most of them baked with little or no oil. If you eat out and find that everything is served with French fries, ask if they have baked potatoes, rice, or pasta.

Avoid eating cakes, cookies, chocolate, corn tortilla chips, and pastries, and resist vending machines and canteens at work. If you find a health foodstore too inconvenient, make your own snacks. Fresh fruit and vegetables are the best things to snack on. Dried fruits, such as apricots, figs, prunes, and raisins, are also a healthier option, although high

in sugar. Try slices of carrot, pieces of cauliflower, scallion, radishes, cucumber, or hard-cooked eggs with a dip, such as lowfat hummus, plain yogurt with herbs, or ready-made lowfat dips.

Slices of apple dipped in honey can be a delicious quick snack if you have a sweet tooth. Sherbets, such as Peach Sherbet (see page 230), make a good lowfat alternative to ice cream and are just as delicious on a hot summer's day. You can make muesli bars using rolled oats, and bran muffins and cookies using lowfat ingredients. Instead of chocolate toppings, try making a yogurt topping. Canned fruit is also a good option, although you should avoid fruits that are preserved in syrup. Although there is no fat in syrup, the sugar content is high and natural fruit juice is better.

If you regularly eat take-outs, this is one of the first things to address. Almost everything seems to be deep-fried in saturated fats and is bad for your cholesterol levels, your weight and your heart. Try homemade burgers and you will discover a new taste experience, as well as cutting down your fat intake. Take-out pizza is high in saturated fats and the best thing you can do is make your own at home. If you do end up getting a take-out pizza, blot each slice well with paper towels to soak up excess fat on the surface. You can adapt all sorts of traditional and favorite meals to a lowfat diet, just as you can adapt them for a diabetic, vegetarian, or low-sodium diet.

the lowfat family

Exercise is as important as eating healthily and nobody really has any excuse for not doing some exercise. Walking is one of the best ways to burn off extra fat and calories, and aids digestion. Moderate exercise a little while after a meal is safe, but you shouldn't start a heavy workout soon after eating or you will give yourself indigestion. If you are trying to involve your whole family in a lifestyle change, go for walks together after a lowfat

lunch. A picnic is the ideal setting for a lowfat meal and many recipes in this book are easy to make, pack, and carry. Ideas for picnic nibbles include Trout Mousse (see page 52) with lowfat crackers or breadsticks, or Crudités with Garlic Chive & Cilantro Dip (see page 38). Persuading the family to eat a lowfat diet with you can be difficult. If part of your aim is to lose weight, point out all the benefits to your family.

Be careful about putting children on diets. If your child is overweight, consult your doctor before making any drastic changes in their diet. Children need different amounts of nutrients and are very sensitive to changes in lifestyle. Cutting down on potato chips, chocolate, candies, fast food, and fatty snacks is the first step and this can be done without seeing a doctor first. Children under five years old should not be given skim or lowfat milk or dairy products made from them.

Children will invariably complain about eating vegetables, but if you serve them in an attractive way, perhaps with a dressing, you are more likely to get a positive response. Snacks for children could include breadsticks and dips, homemade potato chips, fruit slices, and fruit kabobs dipped in honey and grilled or broiled (on skewers without sharp points), and homemade lowfat ice cream. Many of these things are a good idea for healthy packed lunches to take to school. Try Scrumptious Sandwiches (see page 62), Vegetable Samosas (see page 86), and Spicy Chicken with Naan (see page 66)—with a little less spice for very young ones.

Many people are very wary of lowfat "diets," yet they often pay little attention to how their evening meal is prepared. If your family is used to steak, egg and French fries smothered in ketchup, serve broiled steak with the fat trimmed off, baked potato with lowfat spread, steamed vegetables or salad and homemade lowfat mayonnaise or tomato chutney. You do not need to tell them that the meal is lowfat—simply serve it up and wait for their requests for a second helping!

basic recipes

vegetable stock

makes: 2 quarts
preparation time: 10 minutes
cooking time: 40 minutes

2 tbsp corn oil
4 oz/115 g onions, finely chopped
4 oz/115 g leeks, finely chopped
4 oz/115 g carrots, finely chopped
4 celery stalks, finely chopped
3 oz/85 g fennel, finely chopped
3 oz/85 g tomatoes, finely chopped
2.25 quarts water
1 bouquet garni

1 Heat the oil in a large pan. Add the onions and leeks and cook over low heat, stirring occasionally, for 5 minutes, or until softened.

2 Add the remaining vegetables, cover, and cook over low heat, stirring occasionally, for 10 minutes. Add the water and bouquet garni, bring to a boil and let simmer for 20 minutes.

3 Strain, cool, and store in the refrigerator. Use immediately or freeze in portions for up to 3 months.

> ### cook's tip
> To make the bouquet garni, tie 4 fresh parsley stems, 1 clove, 1 bay leaf, and 4 peppercorns in a piece of cheesecloth.

fish stock

makes: 1.3 quarts
preparation time: 10 minutes
cooking time: 30 minutes

1 lb 7 oz/650 g white fish heads, bones and trimmings, rinsed
1 onion, sliced
2 celery stalks, chopped
1 carrot, sliced
1 bay leaf
4 fresh parsley sprigs
4 black peppercorns
½ lemon, sliced

1.3 quarts water
½ cup dry white wine

1 Place the fish heads, bones and trimmings in a large pan. Add the remaining ingredients, then bring to a boil and skim off the foam that rises to the surface with a slotted spoon.

2 Reduce the heat, partially cover, and let simmer gently for 25 minutes.

3 Strain the stock, without pressing down on the contents of the strainer. Let cool and store in the refrigerator. Use immediately or freeze in portions for up to 3 months.

> ### variation
> Shellfish stock has a beautifully delicate flavor. Use shrimp heads and shells with white fish trimmings.

chicken stock

makes: 2.5 quarts
preparation time: 15 minutes, plus 30 minutes chilling
cooking time: 3½ hours

3 lb/1.3 kg chicken wings and necks
2 onions, cut into wedges
4 quarts water
2 carrots, coarsely chopped
2 celery stalks, coarsely chopped
10 fresh parsley sprigs
4 fresh thyme sprigs
2 bay leaves
10 black peppercorns

1 Put the chicken and onions in a large, heavy-bottomed pan and cook over low heat, stirring frequently, until lightly browned all over.

2 Add the water and stir to scrape off sediment on the bottom of the pan. Bring to a boil and skim off any foam. Add the remaining ingredients, partially cover, and let simmer gently for 3 hours.

3 Strain, cool, and chill in the refrigerator. When cold, carefully remove and discard the layer of fat that has set on the surface. Use immediately or freeze in portions for up to 6 months.

beef stock

makes: 1.7 quarts
preparation time: 15 minutes, plus 30 minutes chilling
cooking time: 4¼ hours

2 lb 4 oz/1 kg beef marrow bones, sawn into 3-inch/7.5-cm pieces
1 lb 7 oz/650 g stewing beef in 1 piece
2.8 quarts water
4 cloves
2 onions, halved
2 celery stalks, coarsely chopped
8 peppercorns
1 bouquet garni

1 Place the bones in the bottom of a large, heavy-bottomed pan and put the beef on top. Add the water and bring to a boil over low heat, skimming off all the foam that rises to the surface.

2 Press a clove into each onion half and add to the pan with the celery, peppercorns, and bouquet garni. Reduce the heat, partially cover and let simmer very gently for 3 hours. Remove the meat and let simmer for an additional 1 hour.

3 Strain, cool, and chill in the refrigerator. When cold, carefully remove and discard the layer of fat that has set on the surface. Use immediately or freeze in portions for up to 6 months.

lowfat mayonnaise

makes: ¾ cup
preparation time: 10 minutes,
plus 10 minutes standing
cooking time: 0 minutes

4 hard-cooked egg yolks
2 tbsp white wine vinegar
2 tbsp lemon juice
1 tsp Dijon mustard
salt and pepper
4 tbsp lowfat plain yogurt

1 Mix the egg yolks, vinegar, lemon juice, and mustard together, then season to taste with salt and pepper. Mash thoroughly with a fork to blend.

2 Beat in the yogurt, 1 tablespoon at a time, until incorporated.

3 Cover with plastic wrap and let stand for 10 minutes to let the flavors mingle.

saffron sauce

serves: 6
preparation time: 15 minutes
cooking time: 0 minutes

1 egg yolk
pinch of salt
pinch of powdered saffron
¼ tsp ground coriander
¼ tsp ground cumin
½ cup corn oil
1½ tsp white wine vinegar
1½ tsp lemon juice
½ cup lowfat plain yogurt

1 Put the egg yolk in a bowl and beat with the salt, then stir in the saffron, coriander, and cumin.

2 Add the corn oil, one drop at a time, beating constantly. When half the oil has been incorporated, add the remainder in a steady stream, beating constantly.

3 Stir in the vinegar and lemon juice and fold in the yogurt. Cover and let chill in the refrigerator until required.

cook's tip

For a quick and easy lowfat dressing, put 1 tablespoon of honey in a bowl, add 6 tablespoons of lowfat plain yogurt, and beat until blended. Season to taste.

Fat content of common foods

The following figures show the weight of fat in grams per 3½ oz/100 g of each food.

vegetables

Beet, raw	0.1 g
Broccoli	0.9 g
Cabbage	0.4 g
Carrots	0.3 g
Cauliflower	0.9 g
Celery	0.2 g
Cucumber	0.1 g
Eggplant	0.4 g
French fries, homemade	6.7 g
French fries, oven	4.2 g
French fries, ready-made	12.4 g
Mushrooms	0.5 g
Onions	0.2 g
Peas	1.5 g
Potatoes	0.2 g
Tomatoes	0.3 g
Zucchini	0.4 g

beans

Black-eyed peas, cooked	1.8 g
Chickpeas, canned	2.9 g
Lima beans, canned	0.5 g
Hummus	12.6 g
Red kidney beans, canned	0.6 g
Red lentils, cooked	0.4 g

fish and shellfish

Cod fillets, raw	0.7 g
Crab, canned	0.5 g
Crab, cooked	2.0 g
Haddock, raw	0.6 g
Lemon sole, raw	1.5 g
Mussels	2.0 g
Shrimp	0.9 g
Trout, broiled	5.4 g
Tuna, canned in brine	0.6 g
Tuna, canned in oil	9.0 g

meat

Bacon, lean	39.5 g
Beef, ground, raw	16.2 g
Beef, ground, extra lean, raw	9.6 g
Rump steak, trimmed, raw	4.1 g
Lamb, trimmed, raw	8.3 g
Pork, trimmed, raw	4.0 g
Chicken breast portion, raw	1.1 g
Chicken, roasted	12.5 g
Duck, meat only, raw	6.5 g
Duck, roasted	38.1 g
Turkey, meat only, raw	1.6 g

dairy and fats

Brie	26.9 g
Butter	81.7 g
Cheddar	34.4 g
Cheddar, reduced fat	15.0 g
Cream cheese	47.4 g
Cream, heavy	48.0 g
Cream, heavy, reduced fat	24.0 g
Cream, light	19.1 g
Cream, whipping	39.3 g
Crème fraîche	40.0 g
Crème fraîche, reduced fat	15.0 g
Edam	25.4 g
Feta	20.2 g
Lowfat spread	40.5 g
Lowfat spread, very	25.0 g
Margarine	81.6 g
Milk, whole	3.9 g
Milk, skim	0.1 g
Parmesan	32.7 g
Shortening	99.0 g
Skim milk soft cheese	trace
Yogurt, low fat	0.8 g
Yogurt, strained plain	9.1 g
Yogurt, reduced fat, strained plain	5.0 g

oils

Corn oil	99.9 g
Olive oil	99.9 g
Safflower oil	99.9 g

eggs

Whole egg	10.8 g
Egg yolk	30.5 g
Egg white	trace

dressings

Fat free dressing	1.2 g
Mayonnaise	75.6 g
Mayonnaise, reduced calorie	28.1 g
Vinaigrette	49.4 g

cereals and baking

Bread, brown	2.0 g
Bread, white	1.9 g
Bread, whole-wheat	2.5 g
Chocolate, milk	30.7 g
Chocolate, semisweet	28.0 g
Cornflakes	0.7 g
Croissants	20.3 g
Digestive cookies	20.9 g
Digestive cookies, reduced fat	16.4 g
Doughnut, jelly	14.5 g
Sponge cake, fat free	6.1 g
Flour, white	1.3 g
Flour, whole-wheat	2.2 g
Madeira cake	16.9 g
Muesli	5.9 g
Naan bread	12.5 g
Oat crunch bars	26.6 g
Pasta, white, uncooked	1.8 g
Pasta, whole-wheat, uncooked	2.5 g
Pita bread	1.2 g
Raisin bran	1.6 g
Rice, brown, uncooked	2.8 g
Rice, white, uncooked	3.6 g
Shortbread	26.1 g
Sugar, white	0.3 g

preserves

Honey	0 g
Jelly	0.26 g
Lemon curd	5.0 g

processed foods

Baked beans in tomato sauce	0.6 g
Burger, broiled	14.0 g
Burger, fried	17.0 g
Salami	45.2 g
Sausages	22.0 g
Sausages, low fat	6.0 g
Sausage roll	36.4 g

fruit

Apples, eating	0.1 g
Apricots	0.1 g
Avocados	19.5 g
Bananas	0.3 g
Cherries	0.1 g
Currants, black/red/white	1.0 g
Dried mixed fruit	0.4 g
Grapefruit	0.1 g
Olives, in brine	11.0 g
Oranges	0.1 g
Peaches	0.1 g
Pears	0.1 g
Prunes	0.2 g

nuts

Almonds	55.8 g
Brazil nuts	68.2 g
Hazelnuts	63.5 g
Peanuts, plain	46.1 g
Peanut butter	53.7 g
Pine nuts	68.6 g
Walnuts	68.5 g

soups & appetizers

Few things are simpler and more delicious than homemade soup. The recipes here range from winter warmers for family suppers to chilled summer soup, as well as delicately flavored elegant soups to grace a dinner party table. The secret of success lies in using a well-made, flavorsome stock. An added advantage of homemade stock (see page 11) is that you have total control over what goes into it and you can be sure to skim off every last trace of fat from the surface once it has been chilled. You can, of course, use bouillon cubes or bouillon powder, but do read the labels carefully before buying and try to find a brand that is not too salty.

The appetizers featured in this chapter include a mouthwatering selection of vegetarian specialities, as well as delicious dishes with fish, shellfish, chicken and prosciutto—and most of them with fewer than ¼ oz (10 g) of fat per serving. Some require no cooking at all and can be assembled in moments, while others are more elaborate and extravagant dishes for special occasions. There are tempting treats for every time of year, from wonderful ways with summery asparagus (see pages 44 and 48) to the spectacular Oysters Rockefeller (see page 55) for when there's an "r" in the month, as well as any-time dishes, from easy Antipasto Mushrooms (see page 35) to sophisticated Trout Mousse (see page 52).

consommé

serves 4   **prep: 15 mins, plus 1 hr standing**   **cook: 1 hr 15 mins**

*A traditional clear soup made from beef bones and lean beef.
Thin strips of vegetables provide a colorful garnish and if served
with Melba toast it makes the perfect start to any dinner party.*

INGREDIENTS

5½ cups strong Beef Stock (see page 11)

1 cup extra lean fresh ground beef

2 tomatoes, peeled, seeded, and chopped

2 large carrots, chopped

1 large onion, chopped

2 celery stalks, chopped

1 turnip, chopped (optional)

1 bouquet garni

2 egg whites

shells of 2 eggs, crushed

salt and pepper

1–2 tbsp sherry (optional)

Melba toast, to serve (optional)

TO GARNISH

julienne strips of raw carrot,
turnip, celery, or celery root

NUTRITIONAL INFORMATION

Calories 109

Protein 13g

Carbohydrate 7g

Sugars 6g

Fat 3g

Saturates 1g

variation

For the garnish, replace the julienne strips of raw vegetables with a one-egg omelet, cut into thin strips.

cook's tip

You will find it much easier to whisk the consommé hard when it has reached to almost boiling point if you use a balloon whisk.

1 Place the Beef Stock and ground beef in a large, heavy-bottom pan and let stand for 1 hour. Add the tomatoes, carrots, onion, celery, turnip, if using, bouquet garni, egg whites, the crushed shells of 2 eggs, and plenty of salt and pepper and bring to almost boiling point, whisking hard all the time with a whisk.

2 Cover and let simmer for 1 hour, taking care not to let the layer of froth on top of the soup break.

3 Pour the soup through a jelly bag or scalded fine cloth, keeping the froth back until the last, then pour the ingredients through the cloth again into a clean pan. The resulting liquid should be clear. Add the sherry, if using, to the soup and reheat gently until hot. Place the garnish in 4 warmed soup bowls and carefully ladle the soup on top. Serve immediately with Melba toast, if you like.

carrot, apple & celery soup

cook: 40 mins   prep: 30 mins   serves 4

NUTRITIONAL INFORMATION

Calories 153

Protein 2g

Carbohydrate 36g

Sugars 34g

Fat 1g

Saturates 0.2g

For this delicious fresh-tasting soup, use your favorite variety of eating apple rather than a cooking variety, which will give too tart a flavor. This soup is the perfect choice for the start of a special-occasion meal or as part of a light lunch.

INGREDIENTS

2 lb/900 g carrots, finely diced

1 medium onion, chopped

3 celery stalks, diced

4 cups Vegetable Stock (see page 11)

3 medium-size eating apples

2 tbsp tomato paste

1 bay leaf

2 tsp superfine sugar

¼ large lemon

salt and pepper

celery leaves, shredded, to garnish

variation

Substitute 1 large potato, peeled and chopped instead of the celery and garnish with a few sprigs of fresh parsley, if you like.

cook's tip

To core whole apples easily, push an all-purpose corer into the stalk end of the apple and twist to cut round the core, then gently pull it out.

1 Place the carrots, onion, and celery in a large pan and add the Vegetable Stock. Bring to a boil, reduce the heat, cover, and let simmer for 10 minutes.

2 Meanwhile, peel, core, and dice 2 of the apples. Add the diced apple, tomato paste, bay leaf, and sugar to the pan and bring to a boil over medium heat. Reduce the heat, partially cover, and let simmer for 20 minutes. Remove and discard the bay leaf.

3 Meanwhile, wash, core, and cut the remaining apple into thin slices, without peeling. Place the apple slices in a small pan and squeeze over the lemon juice. Heat the apple slices gently and let simmer for 1–2 minutes, or until the apple is tender.

4 Drain the apple slices and set aside until required. Place the carrot and apple mixture in a blender or food processor and process until smooth. Alternatively, press the mixture through a strainer with the back of a wooden spoon. Gently reheat the soup if necessary and season to taste with salt and pepper. Ladle the soup into 4 warmed bowls, top with the reserved apple slices, and shredded celery leaves, and serve immediately.

chinese noodle soup

serves 4   **prep: 10 mins**   ⏲   **cook: 15 mins** ⏲

This soup has everything going for it—not only is it extremely low in fat, but it takes little time to make, looks intriguing and is a mouthwatering combination of flavors and textures.

INGREDIENTS

5 cups Vegetable Stock
(see page 11)
2 tbsp light soy sauce
1½ tsp saffron threads
4 scallions
2 zucchinis
2 large tomatoes
1 garlic clove
4 oz/115 g rice noodles
pepper
finely snipped fresh garlic chives,
to garnish

NUTRITIONAL INFORMATION	
Calories 135	
Protein 3g	
Carbohydrate 29g	
Sugars 3g	
Fat .1g	
Saturates 0g	

variation

To give the soup a spicy lift, season with 1–2 pinches of cayenne pepper instead of the ground black pepper.

1 Pour the Vegetable Stock into a large, heavy-bottom pan, add the light soy sauce, then bring the mixture to a boil over medium heat.

2 Put the saffron threads into a mortar and lightly crush with a pestle, then stir the crushed saffron threads into the hot stock.

3 Prepare the vegetables. Using a sharp knife, slice the scallions into rings, then cut the zucchinis into thin sticks, and peel and chop the tomatoes. Chop the garlic finely, then add all the vegetables to the stock with the rice noodles. Bring the soup back to a boil over medium heat, then cover and let simmer for 5 minutes.

4 Season the soup to taste with pepper and ladle into 4 warmed serving bowls. Garnish with finely snipped garlic chives and serve immediately.

spicy vegetable soup

⏲ **cook: 15 mins**   🕒 **prep: 5 mins**   **serves 4**

Wake up the taste buds with a hint of curry spices in this easy-to-prepare vegetable soup. Served as a light lunch with Indian bread, such as chapati or paratha, it is a healthy option.

NUTRITIONAL INFORMATION	
Calories 75	
Protein 3g	
Carbohydrate 8g	
Sugars 5g	
Fat 4g	
Saturates 1g	

INGREDIENTS

1 tbsp corn oil

10 oz/280 g leeks, thinly sliced

2 garlic cloves, finely chopped

½ tsp grated fresh gingerroot

½ tsp ground cumin

½ tsp ground coriander

½ tsp ground turmeric

5 cups Vegetable Stock

(see page 11)

1 lb/450 g tomatoes, finely diced

2 zucchinis, cut into thin sticks

salt and pepper

3 tbsp chopped fresh cilantro, to garnish

1 Heat the oil in a large, heavy-bottom pan. Add the sliced leeks, chopped garlic, and ginger and cook over medium heat, stirring occasionally, for 2 minutes. Stir in the cumin, coriander, and turmeric and cook, stirring constantly, for 30 seconds.

2 Pour in the Vegetable Stock and stir well, then bring the mixture to a boil. Reduce the heat, cover, and let simmer for 5 minutes, then stir in the diced tomatoes and zucchini sticks. Cover and let simmer for an additional 3 minutes.

3 Season the soup to taste with salt and pepper, then ladle into 4 warmed serving bowls. Garnish with the chopped fresh cilantro and serve.

variation

For a more subtle flavor to this soup, substitute ½ teaspoon crushed saffron threads for the ground turmeric.

easy gazpacho

serves 4 **prep: 10 mins,** ⏱ **plus 2 hrs chilling** **cook: 0 mins** ⏱

The perfect choice for alfresco dining, this classic chilled soup is packed with fresh flavors. As no cooking is involved, the vegetables retain their color and their valuable vitamins, and you remain cool in the kitchen.

INGREDIENTS

1 small cucumber, peeled and chopped
2 red bell peppers, seeded and chopped
2 green bell peppers, seeded and chopped
2 garlic cloves, coarsely chopped
1 fresh basil sprig
2½ cups strained tomatoes
1 tbsp extra virgin olive oil
1 tbsp red wine vinegar
1 tbsp balsamic vinegar
1¼ cups Vegetable Stock (see page 11)

2 tbsp lemon juice
salt and pepper

TO SERVE
2 tbsp diced, peeled cucumber
2 tbsp finely chopped red onion
2 tbsp finely chopped red bell pepper
2 tbsp finely chopped green bell pepper
ice cubes
4 fresh basil sprigs
fresh crusty bread

NUTRITIONAL INFORMATION	
Calories	.85
Protein	.3g
Carbohydrate	.11g
Sugars	.10g
Fat	.3g
Saturates	.1g

variation

For a spicier version, add 1 coarsely chopped onion with the cucumber in Step 1 and add 1–2 seeded, finely chopped fresh chiles to the garnishes.

cook's tip

This is a perfect soup to have on a summer picnic. Add the ice cubes to the soup before transferring it to a large flask.

1 Put the cucumber, bell peppers, garlic, and basil in a food processor and process for 1½ minutes. Add the strained tomatoes, olive oil, and both kinds of vinegar and process until smooth.

2 Pour in the Vegetable Stock and lemon juice and stir. Transfer the mixture to a large bowl. Season to taste with salt and pepper. Cover with plastic wrap and let chill in the refrigerator for at least 2 hours.

3 To serve, prepare the cucumber, onion, and bell peppers, then place in small serving dishes or arrange decoratively on a plate. Place ice cubes in 4 large soup bowls. Stir the soup and ladle it into the bowls. Garnish with the basil sprigs and serve with the prepared vegetables and chunks of fresh crusty bread.

parisian pea soup

serves 4   **prep: 10 mins**   **cook: 15–20 mins**

This is one occasion when cooking with just a little amount of butter is worthwhile because of its rather rich flavor.

INGREDIENTS

2 tbsp butter

2 shallots, finely chopped

1 cup shelled peas

2 Boston or 1 small romaine
lettuce, shredded

5 cups Vegetable Stock
(see page 11)

pinch of freshly grated nutmeg

salt and pepper

2–3 tbsp lowfat sour cream (optional)

fresh chives, to garnish

NUTRITIONAL INFORMATION

Calories	148
Protein	8g
Carbohydrate	14g
Sugars	4g
Fat	7g
Saturates	4g

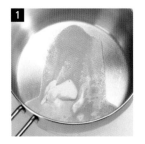

cook's tip

Using homemade Chicken Stock (see page 11) instead of the Vegetable Stock gives this delicate soup a fuller flavor, but also increases the amount of fat slightly.

1 Melt the butter in a large, heavy-bottom pan. Add the shallots and cook over medium heat, stirring occasionally, for 5 minutes, or until softened.

2 Add the peas, shredded lettuce, and stock to the pan and season to taste with nutmeg, salt and pepper. Bring to a boil, then reduce the heat, cover, and let simmer for 10–15 minutes, or until the peas are tender.

3 Remove the pan from the heat and let cool slightly. Transfer the mixture to a blender or food processor and process until a smooth purée forms. Return the soup to the rinsed-out pan and heat through gently until hot. Ladle the soup into 4 large, warmed serving bowls. Top with a spoonful of sour cream, if using, garnish with a few fresh chives and serve.

lentil & tomato soup

cook: 50 mins   **prep: 20 mins**   serves 4

*This fresh-tasting and colorful soup is substantial enough to serve
on its own with some crusty fresh bread for a light lunch or supper.*

NUTRITIONAL INFORMATION	
Calories	.158
Protein	.9g
Carbohydrate	.24g
Sugars	6g
Fat	.4g
Saturates	.1g

INGREDIENTS

1 tbsp corn oil

1 onion, finely chopped

1 garlic glove, crushed

½ tsp ground cumin

½ tsp ground coriander

**1 lb/450 g tomatoes, peeled, seeded,
and chopped**

¾ cup split red lentils

**5 cups Vegetable Stock
(see page 11)**

salt and pepper

**finely chopped fresh cilantro,
to garnish**

cook's tip

Always season lentils with
salt after they have been
cooked, otherwise they will
become tough and may
spoil the finished dish.

1 Heat the oil in a large
pan. Add the onion and
cook over low heat, stirring
occasionally, for 5 minutes, or
until softened.

2 Stir in the garlic, cumin,
ground coriander,
tomatoes, and lentils and
cook, stirring constantly, for an
additional 4 minutes. Pour in
the Vegetable Stock, bring to a

boil, then reduce the heat
and let simmer gently for
30–40 minutes, or until the
lentils are tender. Season to
taste with salt and pepper.

3 Remove the pan from
the heat and let cool
slightly, then transfer the
mixture to a blender or food
processor and process until a
smooth purée forms. Return

the soup to the rinsed-out pan
and reheat gently until hot.
Ladle the soup into 4 large,
warmed soup bowls, garnish
with chopped fresh cilantro
and serve immediately.

mushroom & ginger soup

⏱ cook: 15 mins

🕐 prep: 10 mins, plus
30 mins soaking (optional)

serves 4

variation

Replace the dried Chinese mushrooms with 4½ oz/125 g fresh portobello or cremini mushrooms, sliced, if you prefer.

Thai soups are very quickly and easily put together, and are cooked so that each ingredient can still be tasted in the finished dish.

INGREDIENTS

⅛ cup dried Chinese mushrooms

4 cups hot Vegetable Stock (see page 11)

4½ oz/125 g thread egg noodles

2 tsp corn oil

3 garlic cloves, crushed

1-inch/2.5-cm piece fresh gingerroot, finely shredded

½ tsp mushroom ketchup

1 tsp light soy sauce

4½ oz/125 g bean sprouts

fresh cilantro sprigs, to garnish

cook's tip

Rice noodles are already cooked so only need minimum cooking. They contain no fat and are ideal for anyone on a lowfat diet.

1 Soak the dried Chinese mushrooms, if using, for at least 30 minutes in 1¼ cups of the hot Vegetable Stock. Remove the stalks and discard, then slice the mushrooms. Set aside the stock. Cook the noodles in boiling water for 2–3 minutes, then drain and rinse. Set aside until required.

2 Heat the corn oil in a preheated wok or large, heavy-bottom skillet over high heat. Add the garlic and ginger, stir and add the mushrooms. Stir over high heat for 2 minutes.

3 Add the remaining Vegetable Stock with the reserved stock and bring to a boil. Add the mushroom ketchup and soy sauce. Stir in the bean sprouts and cook until tender. Place some cooked noodles into each soup bowl and ladle the soup on top. Garnish with a few fresh cilantro sprigs and serve immediately.

fragrant chicken soup

serves 4　　　　　**prep: 10 mins** ⊙　　　　　**cook: 15 mins** ⊙

This fiery soup is very popular in Thailand, where it is often sold from roadside stalls as a snack. If you prefer a milder flavor, reduce the number of chiles or choose a milder variety.

INGREDIENTS

2 lemon grass stalks

1¾ cups coconut milk

3 kaffir lime leaves, torn into small pieces

2-inch/5-cm piece galangal or fresh gingerroot, sliced

3 cups water

1 lb 2 oz/500 g skinless, boneless chicken breasts, trimmed of all visible fat and cut into thin strips

8 oz/225 g shiitake mushrooms, chopped

2 tomatoes, cut into wedges

3 fresh Thai chiles, seeded and thinly sliced

3 tbsp lime juice

2 tbsp Thai fish sauce (nam pla)

fresh cilantro leaves, to garnish

NUTRITIONAL INFORMATION

Calories	.190
Protein	.30g
Carbohydrate	.8g
Sugars	.7g
Fat	.5g
Saturates	.2g

variation

You could also make this soup with shelled, raw jumbo shrimp or, for a vegetarian alternative, use cubes of firm tofu instead of the chicken strips.

cook's tip

Be careful when handling fresh chiles, as they can burn. Wearing rubber gloves is a wise precaution and you should always wash your hands thoroughly afterward.

1 Prepare the lemon grass. Remove the tough outer leaves and, using a sharp knife, slice diagonally into chunks.

2 Pour the coconut milk into a large, heavy-bottom pan, add the lemon grass, kaffir lime leaves, and galangal. Bring to a boil, then reduce the heat and let simmer for 2 minutes. Add the water and bring back to a boil. Add the chicken strips, mushrooms, and tomatoes and let simmer for 5 minutes, or until the chicken is tender.

3 Stir in the chiles, lime juice, and Thai fish sauce. Using a slotted spoon, remove and discard the lemon grass and galangal. Ladle the soup into 4 large, warmed soup bowls, garnish with a few fresh cilantro leaves, and serve immediately.

cock-a-leekie soup

cook: 2 hrs   **prep: 30 mins**   **serves 4–6**

NUTRITIONAL INFORMATION

Calories	.45
Protein	.5g
Carbohydrate	.5g
Sugars	.4g
Fat	.1g
Saturates	0.2g

variation

You can replace the Chicken Stock with 3 chicken bouillon cubes dissolved in the same amount of water, if you prefer.

A traditional Scottish soup in which a whole chicken is cooked with the vegetables to add extra flavor to the stock. In some areas, the soup was eaten as a first course, then the cooked chicken was served as part of the main course.

INGREDIENTS

2 lb 4 oz–3 lb 5 oz/1–1.5 kg oven-ready chicken, plus giblets, if available

7–8 cups Chicken Stock (see page 11)

1 onion, sliced

4 leeks, thinly sliced

pinch of ground allspice or ground coriander

1 bouquet garni

salt and pepper

12 no-soak dried prunes, halved and pitted

warm crusty bread, to serve

cook's tip

If no-soak dried prunes are not available, then use dried prunes instead. Place 12 dried prunes in a bowl and pour over enough water to cover. Let soak overnight.

1 Place the chicken, giblets, if using, Chicken Stock, and onion in a large, heavy-bottom pan. Bring to a boil and skim off any scum that rises to the surface with a slotted spoon.

2 Add the leeks, ground allspice or coriander, and the bouquet garni to the pan, season to taste with salt and pepper, cover, and let simmer for 1½ hours, or until the chicken flesh is falling off the bones. Remove the chicken and bouquet garni from the pan and skim off any fat from the surface of the soup.

3 Chop some of the chicken flesh and return to the pan. Add the prunes, return to a boil, and let simmer, uncovered, for 20 minutes. Taste and adjust the seasoning, if necessary. Ladle into a large, warmed soup tureen and serve immediately with warm crusty bread.

rosy melon & strawberries

serves 4   **prep: 10 mins, plus 2 hrs**   **cook: 0 mins**
15 mins chilling/standing

The delicate combination of sweet melon and fresh strawberries macerated in rosé wine and a hint of rose water is a delightful start to a special meal. Always wash rose petals thoroughly and check that they are free from any blemishes and pesticides.

INGREDIENTS

¼ honeydew melon

½ cantaloupe melon

⅔ cup rosé wine

2–3 tsp rose water

generous ½ cup small strawberries, washed and hulled

rose petals, to garnish

NUTRITIONAL INFORMATION

Calories 59

Protein 1g

Carbohydrate 8g

Sugars 8g

Fat 0g

Saturates 20g

variation

Other varieties of melon can also be used in this recipe. Try Galia and charentais instead.

cook's tip

Rose water for culinary use is generally available from large pharmacies and leading supermarkets as well as from more specialist food suppliers.

1 Scoop out the seeds from both melons with a spoon. Using a sharp knife, carefully remove the skin, taking care not to remove too much flesh.

2 Cut the melon flesh into thin strips and place in a large bowl. Pour over the wine and enough rose water to taste. Mix together gently, cover with plastic wrap, and let chill in the refrigerator for at least 2 hours.

3 Halve the strawberries and carefully mix into the melon. Let the melon and strawberries stand at room temperature for 15 minutes to let the flavors develop—if the melon is too cold, there will be little flavor. Arrange on 4 large serving plates and garnish with a few rose petals. Serve immediately.

shrimp-filled artichokes

serves 4

prep: 15 mins, ⏲ **plus 10 mins cooling**

cook: 40–50 mins ⏲

Globe artichokes filled with a delicious stir-fried mix of shrimp, garlic, tomatoes, and scallions make an attractive and adventurous appetizer for a dinner party.

INGREDIENTS

6 tbsp lemon juice

4 globe artichokes

1 tbsp olive or corn oil

6 scallions, finely chopped

1 garlic clove, finely chopped

12 oz/350 g raw shrimp, shelled

6 tomatoes, peeled, seeded, and diced

grated rind of 1 lemon

salt and pepper

grated lemon zest, to garnish

NUTRITIONAL INFORMATION

Calories 172

Protein 25g

Carbohydrate 9g

Sugars 7g

Fat 5g

Saturates 1g

variation

If raw shrimp are not available, use cooked ones instead. Heat them just long enough to warm them through.

1 Fill a large bowl with cold water and add 2 tablespoons of lemon juice.

2 Working on one artichoke at a time, twist off the stalks, cut the bases flat, and pull off any small, tough base leaves. Slice off the tops and trim the tips of the leaves with kitchen scissors. Place in the acidulated water.

3 Bring a large pan of water to a boil, add the remaining lemon juice and the artichokes, cover, and cook for 30–40 minutes, or until a leaf comes away easily from the bases. Remove from the pan and invert to drain. Set aside to cool.

4 Heat the olive oil in a large skillet or preheated wok over medium–high heat. Add the finely chopped scallions and garlic and stir-fry for 3–4 minutes, then add the shrimp and stir-fry for an additional 3 minutes, or until they change color. Stir in the diced tomatoes and lemon rind and season to taste with salt and pepper. Remove the skillet from the heat.

5 When the artichokes are cool enough to handle, remove and discard the chokes. Spoon the stir-fried shrimp into the center of the artichokes and garnish with grated lemon zest. Serve warm.

antipasto mushrooms

⏲ **cook: 30 mins**　　　⏱ **prep: 10 mins, plus 30 mins cooling**　　　**serves 4**

Traditionally, porcini mushrooms, also known as cèpes, would be used for this dish, but you can make it with any of your favorite varieties, such as oyster, chanterelles, and even white mushrooms.

NUTRITIONAL INFORMATION	
Calories	100
Protein	3g
Carbohydrate	2g
Sugars	2g
Fat	9g
Saturates	1g

INGREDIENTS

3 tbsp olive oil

2 garlic cloves, finely chopped

8 oz/225 g tomatoes, peeled, seeded, and finely chopped

1 tbsp finely chopped fresh oregano

salt and pepper

1 lb 2 oz/500 g open-cap and closed cup mushrooms

fresh flatleaf parsley sprigs, to garnish

crusty bread, to serve

cook's tip

If you want to use dried porcini mushrooms, soak 1 tablespoon mushrooms in boiling water for 20 minutes, or until soft. Drain, then add to the rest of the mushrooms in the skillet in Step 2.

1 Heat 1 tablespoon of the olive oil in a large, heavy-bottom pan, add the garlic and cook over low heat, stirring constantly, for 1 minute. Add the tomatoes and oregano and season to taste with salt and pepper. Cook over low heat, stirring frequently, for 20 minutes, or until the mixture is pulpy and thickened.

2 Using a sharp knife, slice the mushrooms thinly. Heat the remaining olive oil in a large skillet. Add the mushrooms and cook over medium heat, stirring frequently, for 5 minutes, or until tender. Stir the mushrooms into the tomato mixture and season with salt. Reduce the heat, cover, and let simmer for an additional 10 minutes.

3 Transfer the mushroom mixture to a bowl and let cool. Transfer to a large serving dish, garnish with flatleaf parsley and serve at room temperature with crusty bread.

mexican vegetable platter

serves 4   **prep: 10 mins,**   **cook: 8 mins**
plus 40 mins chilling

Known as pico de gallo, *this tempting selection of chilled vegetables and fruit is served with a spicy red bell pepper and chile purée. It makes a refreshing appetizer to a summer supper.*

INGREDIENTS

2 tsp corn oil	7 oz/200 g carrots
1 red bell pepper, seeded and diced	1 cucumber
juice of 1 small orange	½ pineapple
juice of 1 lime	1 mango
1–2 fresh red chiles, seeded and finely chopped	½ bunch of fresh mint

---

NUTRITIONAL INFORMATION

Calories	.96
Protein	.2g
Carbohydrate	.19g
Sugars	.18g
Fat	.2g
Saturates	.0g

---

variation

Other vegetables and fruit can be used. Include slices of avocado, brushed with lime juice to prevent discoloration, and chunks of papaya.

---

cook's tip

Choose firm, slightly underripe mangoes, which slice easily. Using a sharp knife, peel the mango completely, then carefully slice around the stone.

1 First, make the pepper purée. Heat the corn oil in a large skillet and add the bell pepper. Cook over medium heat, stirring occasionally for 2 minutes. Add the orange and lime juice and cook for an additional 5 minutes. Remove from the heat and let cool slightly, then transfer to a blender or food processor and process until a smooth purée forms. Transfer to a small serving bowl and add the chiles. Cover with plastic wrap and let chill in the refrigerator until ready to serve.

2 Peel the carrots and cut into thin diagonal slices. Peel the cucumber, cut in half and, using a teaspoon, scoop out the seeds, then thinly slice.

3 Cut the plume off the pineapple and discard. Cut the pineapple into quarters, lengthwise. Stand the quarters upright and cut away the central core. Slice off the skin with a sharp knife, remove any eyes, and cut into cubes. Peel the mango and slice the flesh. Discard the stone. Arrange the fruit and vegetables decoratively on a large serving plate. Cover and let chill in the refrigerator for 15 minutes.

4 Slice or tear the mint leaves into thin strips. Spoon the pepper purée over the chilled vegetables, sprinkle with the mint, and serve.

crudités with garlic chive & cilantro dip

serves 4   **prep: 10 mins** ☽   **cook: 2 mins** ⏱

Raw vegetables are the ideal healthy start to a meal, but creamy dips can undo all your good intentions. This is the perfect solution—all the richness and flavor, but none of the fat.

INGREDIENTS

CRUDITÉS	DIP
4 oz/115 g baby corn	1 tbsp hot water
4 oz/115 g young asparagus	1 tsp saffron threads
spears, trimmed	1 cup fat free mascarpone cheese
1 head of chicory, leaves separated	3 tbsp chopped fresh cilantro
1 red bell pepper, seeded and sliced	1 tbsp snipped fresh garlic chives
1 orange bell pepper, seeded and sliced	salt and pepper
8 radishes, trimmed	fresh cilantro sprigs, to garnish

NUTRITIONAL INFORMATION

Calories 67

Protein 7g

Carbohydrate 9g

Sugars 8g

Fat 1g

Saturates 0g

variation

Try using different selections of vegetables, such as celery stalks, trimmed scallions, strips of cucumber, and thin carrot sticks.

cook's tip

Fat free mascarpone cheese is great for dips because it is soft and is easily mixed with other ingredients. If you cannot find it, use lowfat plain yogurt instead.

1 Blanch the corn and asparagus in separate pans of boiling water for 2 minutes. Drain, plunge into ice water, and drain again. Arrange all the vegetables on a serving platter and cover with a damp dish towel.

2 For the dip, put the water in a small bowl. Lightly crush the saffron threads between your fingers and add to the bowl, then let stand for 3–4 minutes, or until the water is a rich golden color.

3 Put the mascarpone cheese in a separate bowl and beat until smooth, then beat in the infused saffron water. Stir in the chopped cilantro and snipped chives and season to taste with salt and pepper. Transfer to a serving bowl and garnish with a few sprigs of fresh cilantro. Serve immediately with the prepared vegetables.

bruschetta

cook: 5 mins

prep: 15 mins, plus 30 mins standing

serves 4

NUTRITIONAL INFORMATION

Calories	161
Protein	. . . . .1g
Carbohydrate	. . . . .20g
Sugars	. . . . .161g
Fat	. . . . .1g
Saturates	. . . . .20g

Traditionally, this Italian savory is enriched with olive oil. Here, sun-dried tomatoes are a good substitute and only a little oil is used.

INGREDIENTS

2¼ oz/60 g dry-pack sun-dried tomatoes

1¼ cups boiling water

14-inch/35-cm long whole-wheat stick of French bread

1 large garlic clove, halved

2 tbsp pitted black olives in brine, drained and quartered

2 tsp olive oil

salt and pepper

2 tbsp chopped fresh basil

1½ oz/40 g grated lowfat mozzarella cheese

TO GARNISH

shredded fresh basil leaves

fresh basil sprigs

variation

Make your own topping, such as cherry tomatoes, capers, a few shavings of fresh Parmesan cheese, and fresh tarragon leaves to garnish.

cook's tip

If you use sun-dried tomatoes packed in oil, drain them, rinse in warm water, and drain again on paper towels. Though less rich in flavor, thinly sliced fresh tomatoes can be used instead.

1 Place the sun-dried tomatoes in a small heatproof bowl and pour over the boiling water. Let stand for 30 minutes to soften. Drain well and pat dry with paper towels. Slice into thin strips and set aside.

2 Preheat the broiler to medium. Trim and discard the ends of the bread and cut into 12 slices. Arrange on a broiler rack and cook under the preheated broiler for 1–2 minutes on each side until golden. Rub both sides of each piece of bread with the cut sides of the garlic. Top with strips of sun-dried tomato and olives.

3 Brush lightly with olive oil and season well with salt and pepper. Sprinkle with the chopped fresh basil and grated mozzarella cheese and return to the broiler for 1–2 minutes, or until the cheese is melted and bubbling. Transfer to a warmed serving platter and garnish with shredded basil leaves and sprigs of basil. Serve immediately.

parsley, chicken & ham pâté

serves 4 **prep: 25 mins,** ⏲ **plus 30 mins chilling** **cook: 0 mins** ⏲

Pâté is easy to make at home, and this combination of lean chicken and ham mixed with herbs is especially straightforward.

INGREDIENTS

8 oz/225 g skinless, boneless, lean chicken, cooked

3½ oz/100 g lean ham

small bunch of fresh parsley

1 garlic clove, peeled

1 tsp grated lime rind

2 tbsp lime juice

½ cup lowfat mascarpone cheese

salt and pepper

lime zest, to garnish

TO SERVE

lime wedges

crisp bread or Melba toast

NUTRITIONAL INFORMATION	
Calories 119	
Protein 20g	
Carbohydrate 2g	
Sugars 2g	
Fat 3g	
Saturates 1g	

variation

This pâté can also be made with ground, lean, cooked turkey, beef, or pork, or with shrimp, white crabmeat, or tuna.

1 Finely chop the chicken, ham, parsley, and garlic and place in a large bowl, then mix together.

2 Add the lime rind and juice and mix well. Alternatively, finely chop the chicken and ham and place in a blender or food processor. Finely chop the parsley and garlic and add to the blender

or food processor with the lime rind and juice and process until finely ground. Transfer the mixture to a large bowl.

3 Using a metal spoon, mix in the mascarpone cheese, then season to taste with salt and pepper, cover with plastic wrap and let chill in the refrigerator for 30 minutes.

4 Pile the pâté into individual serving dishes and garnish with lime zest. Serve the pâtés with lime wedges and crisp bread.

spinach cheese molds

cook: 50 mins   **prep: 50 mins, plus 1 hr chilling**   serves 4

These flavor-packed little molds are a perfect appetizer for a special-occasion meal or as a light lunch. Serve with warmed pita bread.

NUTRITIONAL INFORMATION	
Calories	119
Protein	. . . . .6g
Carbohydrate	. . . . .2g
Sugars	. . . . .2g
Fat	. . . . .9g
Saturates	. . . . .6g

INGREDIENTS

generous 2 cups fresh spinach leaves

generous 1¼ cups skim milk soft cheese

2 garlic cloves, crushed

few sprigs of fresh parsley, finely chopped

salt and pepper

TO SERVE

salad greens and fresh herbs

warmed pita bread

variation

Replace the chopped fresh parsley with fresh tarragon or chives. A mix of all of these herbs would work equally well.

1 Trim the stalks from the spinach leaves and discard, then rinse the leaves thoroughly under cold running water. Pack the wet leaves into a small pan, cover, and cook for 3–4 minutes, or until wilted. Drain and pat dry with paper towels. Line the bases of 4 small ovenproof bowls or individual ramekins with parchment paper, then line the

bowls or ramekins with the wilted spinach leaves so that the leaves overhang the edges of the bowls.

2 Place the cheese in a small bowl and add the crushed garlic and chopped fresh parsley. Mix together thoroughly until blended, then season to taste with salt and pepper.

3 Spoon the cheese and herb mixture into the prepared bowls or ramekins and cover the cheese with the overhanging spinach. Alternatively, lay extra leaves to cover the top. Place a waxed paper circle on top of each dish and weigh down with a 3½ oz/100 g weight. Let chill in the refrigerator for 1 hour.

4 Remove the weights and peel off the paper. Loosen the molds gently by running a small spatula round the edges of each dish and turn them out onto 4 serving plates. Serve the molds with a mixture of salad greens and fresh herbs, and pita bread.

chicken & asparagus timbales

serves 4   **prep: 15–20 mins,** ⟲ **plus 1 hr 10 mins chilling**   **cook: 30 mins**

These elegant little molds would make a wonderful appetizer for a dinner party. They are packed with flavor, yet light and melt-in-the-mouth, and they look quite stunning. Although they take some time and effort to prepare, the results are worth it.

INGREDIENTS

1 lemon	4 oz/115 g young asparagus
2 skinless, boneless chicken	spears, trimmed
breasts, about 4 oz/115 g each,	2 tbsp white wine
trimmed of all visible fat	1 envelope powdered gelatin
2 fresh tarragon sprigs	½ cup fat free mascarpone cheese
⅔ cup water	1 tsp chopped fresh tarragon
salt and pepper	

NUTRITIONAL INFORMATION

Calories 92
Protein 15g
Carbohydrate 2g
Sugars 2g
Fat 2g
Saturates 1g

variation

Substitute fresh rosemary or thyme instead of tarragon, but use them sparingly as they have an intense flavor and may overwhelm the dish.

cook's tip

When heating gelatin over a pan of simmering water, make sure that the gelatin does not boil as it will become stringy and will spoil the finished dish.

1 Cut a strip of rind from the lemon. Squeeze the juice and set aside. Put the lemon rind, chicken, tarragon sprigs, and water in a pan and season to taste. Cover, bring to a boil, then reduce the heat to low and cook for 20 minutes, or until tender. Remove the chicken with a slotted spoon and cool. Strain and set aside the cooking liquid. Blanch the asparagus for 5 minutes. Drain, then cut off and set aside 1½ inches/4 cm of the tips. Chop the stalks.

2 Put the reserved cooking liquid in a measuring cup. Make up to ⅔ cup with water, if necessary. Stir in the white wine. Put 4 tablespoons of the mixture in a heatproof bowl, sprinkle ½ teaspoon of gelatin on top, let stand for 2 minutes, then set over a pan of simmering water. Stir for 2–3 minutes. Divide between 4 ramekins and let chill for 5 minutes. Arrange 2 asparagus tips, facing in opposite directions, in each ramekin and chill until set. Dissolve the remaining gelatin in the remaining stock and wine, as before.

3 Chop the chicken, then process in a food processor until smooth. Add the lemon juice, mascarpone cheese, and gelatin mixture and mix. Transfer to a bowl, stir in the asparagus stalks and tarragon. Season. Divide between the ramekins and let chill for 1 hour, or until set. Dip the base of the ramekins in hot water and invert onto 4 plates.

chinese pot stickers

serves 6   **prep: 30 mins**   **cook: 50–60 mins**

These tasty chicken- and vegetable-filled dumplings are equally suitable for serving as part of a Chinese meal or as an appetizer before a Western main course. You can also serve them with plain dark soy sauce or chili sauce for dipping, if you like.

INGREDIENTS

6 oz/175 g Chinese leaves, shredded

4 cups boiling water

½ cup lean ground chicken

5 canned water chestnuts, drained, rinsed, and chopped

1 scallion, finely chopped

1 tablespoon Chinese rice wine

1 teaspoon light soy sauce

1 tsp cornstarch

pepper

24 won ton skins, thawed if frozen

peanut or corn oil, for brushing

DIPPING SAUCE

½ cup Vegetable Stock (see page 11)

1 tbsp superfine sugar

3 tbsp dark soy sauce

NUTRITIONAL INFORMATION

Calories 109

Protein 7g

Carbohydrate 19g

Sugars 4g

Fat 1g

Saturates 0g

variation

You can substitute the same quantity of lean ground steak or chopped shelled raw shrimp for the chicken, if you like.

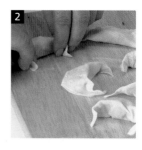

cook's tip

Cook the pot stickers in batches, as they should not touch each other during the process. When steaming, add enough water to come about halfway up the sides of the pot stickers.

1 First make the dipping sauce by mixing all the ingredients in a small bowl, stirring until the sugar has dissolved, and set aside.

2 Put the Chinese leaves in a colander and pour over the boiling water. Drain well, pressing the leaves with the back of a spoon. Transfer the Chinese leaves to a large bowl with the chicken, water chestnuts, scallion, Chinese rice wine, soy sauce, and cornstarch. Season to taste with pepper and mix well. Spread out 1 won ton skin and place a teaspoon of the filling in the center. Brush the edge with water and fold to make a half moon. Press the edges together to seal and crimp the rim slightly. Gently curve the dumpling by pinching the ends of the rim between your index fingers and thumbs. Make the remaining dumplings in the same way.

3 Brush the bottom of a nonstick wok or skillet with peanut oil and set over medium heat. Add 5–6 dumplings in a single layer, smooth sides downward. Cook for 2–3 minutes, or until golden brown underneath. Add 3–4 tablespoons water, partially cover, and steam for 10 minutes, or until cooked through and most of the water has evaporated. Transfer to a serving plate and keep warm. Cook the remaining dumplings, in batches, in the same way. Serve immediately with the dipping sauce.

asparagus with orange dressing

serves 4　　　　**prep: 10 mins,** 🕒　　　　**cook: 10 mins** 🕒
plus 15 mins standing

Asparagus is in season for only a short time and is a special treat in late spring and early summer. Imported asparagus is available all year round, but it may be very expensive.

INGREDIENTS

2 oranges

12 oz/350 g asparagus, trimmed

1 tablespoon lemon juice

1 scallion, finely chopped

1 garlic clove, finely chopped

2 tbsp extra virgin olive oil

1 tbsp white wine vinegar

NUTRITIONAL INFORMATION	
Calories	.88
Protein	.3g
Carbohydrate	.6g
Sugars	.6g
Fat	.6g
Saturates	.1g

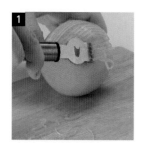

cook's tip

A special asparagus kettle is designed so that the stems cook in the water while the tips are steamed. If you don't have one, use a deep pan, tie the asparagus loosely and wedge upright.

1 Bring a small pan of water to a boil over medium heat. Using a zester, cut the rind of both oranges into very thin strips. Set aside the oranges. Add the rind to the pan, return the mixture to a boil and let simmer for 1 minute. Drain the rind, refresh under cold running water, and drain again, then set aside.

2 Bring a large pan of water to a boil over medium heat. Add the asparagus and cook for 5 minutes, or until just tender. Drain the asparagus, refresh under cold running water, and drain again. Pat dry with paper towels. Arrange the asparagus on a serving dish, cover with plastic wrap, and let chill in the refrigerator until required.

3 To make the orange dressing, squeeze the reserved oranges to make 5 tablespoons of orange juice. Mix the orange juice, lemon juice, scallion, garlic, and orange rind together in a small bowl, then let stand at room temperature for 15 minutes to let all the flavors mingle. Using a balloon whisk, whisk in the olive oil and

vinegar. Pour the dressing over the asparagus and serve immediately.

prosciutto with figs

cook: 0 mins　　　**prep: 10 mins, plus 20 mins chilling**　　　serves 4

This classic Italian appetizer couldn't be easier or more delicious. Prosciutto has a uniquely aromatic flavor and is served in paper-thin slices. Succulent fresh figs make a natural partnership.

NUTRITIONAL INFORMATION	
Calories	124
Protein	13g
Carbohydrate	6g
Sugars	5g
Fat	6g
Saturates	2g

INGREDIENTS

6 oz/175 g prosciutto, thinly sliced

pepper

4 fresh figs

1 lime

2 fresh basil sprigs

variation

This dish is also delicious made with 4 slices of charentais melon or 12–16 cooked and cooled asparagus spears, instead of the figs.

1 Using a sharp knife, trim the visible fat from the slices of prosciutto and discard. Arrange the prosciutto on 4 large serving plates, loosely folding it so that it falls into decorative shapes. Season to taste with pepper.

2 Using a sharp knife, cut each fig lengthwise into 4 wedges. Arrange a fig on each serving plate. Cut the lime into 6 wedges, place a wedge on each plate and reserve the others. Remove the leaves from the basil sprigs and divide between the plates. Cover with plastic wrap and let chill in the refrigerator until ready to serve.

3 Just before serving, remove the plates from the refrigerator and squeeze the juice from the remaining lime wedges over the ham.

crab cakes with salsa verde

serves 4 **prep: 15 mins,** ⟲ **plus 30–60 mins chilling** **cook: 15 mins** ⏱

These spicy fish cakes are popular throughout Thailand, where they are eaten as between-meal snacks. Mixing crabmeat with white fish makes the cakes easier to handle and the dish more economical.

INGREDIENTS

1¾ cups crabmeat, thawed if frozen

9 oz/250 g white fish fillet, such as cod, skinned and coarsely chopped

1 fresh red chile, seeded and coarsely chopped

1 garlic clove, coarsely chopped

1-inch/2.5-cm piece of fresh gingerroot, coarsely chopped

1 lemon grass stalk, coarsely chopped

3 tbsp chopped fresh cilantro

1 egg white

peanut or corn oil, for frying

SALSA VERDE

2 fresh green chiles, seeded and coarsely chopped

8 scallions, coarsely chopped

2 garlic cloves, coarsely chopped

1 bunch of fresh parsley

grated rind and juice of 1 lime

juice of 1 lemon

4 tbsp olive oil

1 tbsp green Tabasco sauce

salt and pepper

NUTRITIONAL INFORMATION

Calories 318

Protein 26g

Carbohydrate 2g

Sugars 1g

Fat 23g

Saturates 3g

variation

For an elegant presentation, garnish the crab cakes with fresh Chinese chives. If these are unavailable, use ordinary fresh chives instead.

cook's tip

Much of the fat in this recipe is contained in the salsa verde dip, so if you would prefer a lower fat dish, serve only small helpings of the salsa verde. The remainder can be stored in the refrigerator.

1 Place the crabmeat, fish, red chile, garlic, ginger, lemon grass, cilantro, and egg white in a food processor and process until thoroughly blended, then transfer to a bowl, cover with plastic wrap, and let chill in for 30–60 minutes.

2 Meanwhile, make the salsa verde. Put the green chiles, scallions, garlic, and parsley in a food processor and process until finely chopped. Transfer to a small bowl and stir in the lime rind, lime and lemon juice, olive oil, and green Tabasco sauce. Season to taste with salt and pepper, cover with plastic wrap, and let chill in the refrigerator until ready to serve.

3 Heat 2 tablespoons of the peanut oil in a nonstick skillet. Add spoonfuls of the crab mixture, flattening them gently with a spatula and keeping them spaced well apart. Cook for 4 minutes, then turn with a spatula and cook the other side for 3 minutes, or until golden brown. Remove from the skillet and keep warm while you cook the remaining batches, adding more oil if necessary. Transfer the crab cakes to a large serving plate, garnish, and serve with the salsa verde.

trout mousse

serves 6 **prep: 15 mins,** ⏲ **plus 3 hrs 20 mins chilling** **cook: 15 mins** ⏲

This delicate pink mousse makes a superb appetizer for a dinner party or buffet table. Trout is an oily fish, but contains the "good" omega-3 essential fatty acids that are vital for well-being and protect against heart disease and circulatory problems.

INGREDIENTS

⅔ cup Fish Stock (see page 11)

1 tbsp French vermouth

1 tbsp lime juice

1 small onion, finely chopped

9 oz/250 g trout fillets

1 tsp tomato paste

2 tbsp strained plain yogurt

salt and white pepper

1½ tsp water

½ envelope (1½ tsp) powdered gelatin

1 large egg white

fresh dill sprigs, to garnish

Melba toast (see Cook's Tip) or toasted whole-wheat bread, to serve

NUTRITIONAL INFORMATION	
Calories	79
Protein	. . . . .10g
Carbohydrate	. . . . .1g
Sugars	. . . . .1g
Fat	. . . . .4g
Saturates	. . . . .1g

variation

This mousse can also be made with sea trout fillets, which also have pink flesh and a delicate flavor.

cook's tip

To make Melba toast, remove the crusts from slices of bread and broil on both sides. Slice through horizontally to give 2 thin slices. Cut in half diagonally and broil until golden.

1 Pour the Fish Stock into a wide, shallow pan and add the vermouth, lime juice, and onion. Bring to a boil, then reduce the heat to low and let simmer for 3 minutes. Add the fish fillets, skin-side down, cover, and poach for 3 minutes. Remove from the heat and leave, still covered, until cool. Lift out the fish, reserving the stock, then

remove and discard the skin and flake the flesh. Strain the stock into a food processor, add the fish, and process until a smooth paste forms. Transfer to a bowl and beat in the tomato paste and yogurt. Season to taste.

2 Pour the water into a small, heatproof bowl and sprinkle the gelatin on the

surface. Let stand for 2 minutes to soften, then set the bowl over a pan of simmering water and stir for 2–3 minutes, or until the gelatin has dissolved. Pour the gelatin mixture into the fish mixture in a steady stream, beating constantly. Let chill in the refrigerator for 15–20 minutes, or until just starting to set.

3 Whisk the egg white until stiff, but not dry. Gently stir one-quarter of the egg white into the fish mixture, then fold in the remainder. Rinse 6 ramekins or bowls with water and spoon in the fish mixture. Smooth the tops, cover, and let chill in the refrigerator for 2–3 hours, or until set. Garnish with dill sprigs and serve with toast.

artichoke hearts with a warm dressing

serves 4   **prep: 15 mins**   **cook: 45 mins**

Artichoke hearts are truly a luxury and taste superb with this warm nutty dressing. For less fat content, omit the walnut garnish. Serve with fresh crusty bread, if you like.

INGREDIENTS

9 oz/250 g mixed salad greens, such as
red leaf, escarole, and corn salad
6 tbsp lemon juice
4 globe artichokes
5 tbsp Calvados
1 shallot, very finely chopped
pinch of salt
1 tbsp red wine vinegar
3 tbsp walnut oil

TO GARNISH
½ cup shelled walnuts, chopped
1 tbsp finely chopped fresh parsley

NUTRITIONAL INFORMATION	
Calories	287
Protein	7g
Carbohydrate	14g
Sugars	2g
Fat	18g
Saturates	2g

variation

This recipe also works well with good-quality canned or bottled artichoke hearts. Drain and rinse well before using.

1 Place the salad greens in a bowl and set aside. Fill a bowl with cold water and add 2 tablespoons of the lemon juice. Working on one artichoke at a time, twist off the stalks, cut the bases flat, and pull off all the dark outer leaves. Slice the artichokes in half horizontally and discard the top parts. Trim round the bases to remove the outer

dark green layer and place in the acidulated water. Bring a pan of water to a boil, add the remaining lemon juice and the artichokes, cover, and cook for 30–40 minutes, or until tender. Drain, refresh under cold running water, and drain again. Pull off and discard the remaining leaves, slice off and discard the chokes, and set the hearts aside.

2 Pour the Calvados into a small pan, add the shallot and salt and bring to just below boiling point. Reduce the heat, carefully ignite the Calvados, and continue to cook until the flames have died down. Stir in the vinegar and walnut oil and cook, stirring constantly, for 1 minute. Remove the pan from the heat.

3 Spoon half the dressing over the salad greens and toss well to coat. Transfer the salad greens to a large serving plate and top with the artichoke hearts. Spoon the remaining dressing over the artichoke hearts, garnish with the walnuts and parsley, and serve immediately.

oysters rockefeller

🔥 **cook: 10 mins**   🕐 **prep: 30 mins**   **serves 6**

This is a variation of the famous New Orleans dish, which is cooked and served on a bed of rock salt. Although an extravagant indulgence, it makes a spectacular appetizer for a special occasion.

NUTRITIONAL INFORMATION	
Calories	.97
Protein	.13g
Carbohydrate	.6g
Sugars	.3g
Fat	.2g
Saturates	.0g

INGREDIENTS

1 lb/450 g fresh spinach leaves

rock salt

36 fresh oysters in their shells

4 scallions, chopped

2 celery stalks, chopped

3 fresh parsley sprigs

1–2 tbsp lowfat plain yogurt

pinch of cayenne pepper

1 tbsp pastis (see Cook's Tip)

cook's tip

Pastis is an alcoholic drink which is flavored with star anise. It is very popular in the south of France. The best-known brand is Pernod.

1 Preheat the oven to 450°F/230°C. Trim the stalks from the spinach leaves and rinse the leaves under cold running water. Put the wet leaves into a large pan, then cover and cook over medium heat for 3 minutes. Turn the spinach over, cover, and cook for an additional 2 minutes. Drain well, squeezing out as much liquid as possible, then set aside. Cover the bottoms of 2 ovenproof dishes with a ½-inch/1-cm layer of rock salt.

2 Wrap a dish towel around one hand and grasp an oyster, flat shell uppermost. Insert a strong knife into the hinge between the shells and twist to prise them open. Run the blade along the inside of the top shell to sever the upper muscle, then along the inside of the lower shell to cut the lower muscle. Discard the top shells. Shuck the remaining oysters in the same way. Set the shells on the salt layers.

3 Place the spinach, scallions, celery, parsley, yogurt, and cayenne pepper in a food processor and pulse until a smooth purée forms. Transfer to a bowl and stir in the pastis. Cover each oyster with a spoonful of the spinach purée, then bake in the preheated oven for 4 minutes. Serve immediately.

snacks & light meals

*There are many occasions when we feel it is time for a "little something,"
but don't want a complete meal. Many popular snacks and easy "instant" meals—from potato
chips and cookies to pizzas and sausages—are extremely high in fat (as well as salt and sugar),
and it is all too easy to wreck your healthy eating plan. So turn to this chapter, packed with
delicious lowfat snacks and light meals, to solve the problem. There is something for everyone.*

*Need a quick snack to keep you going in the middle of the day? Try one of the
luscious Scrumptious Sandwiches (see page 62). If the kids come home from school hungry and
it's a long way until supper time, make a batch of Falafel (see page 90). Want a light lunch
for guests? How about Cantaloupe & Crab Salad (see page 100)? Need to fuel the family
for an action-packed weekend? Try Mexican Eggs (see page 74). Many of these dishes are also
perfect for school lunch boxes and picnics. Whether you want a hot dish to fill the gap on
a wintery day or to ring the changes with some unusual summer salads,
you are sure to find the perfect healthy choice.*

pasta with lowfat pesto

serves 4 **prep: 5 mins** ⟳ **cook: 8–10 mins** ⟳

Pesto is a wonderfully useful sauce that can be served with all kinds of foods, from pasta to baked potatoes, but its great disadvantage is that it contains over 1¾ oz/50 g fat per serving. You can make this sauce without the addition of lots of olive oil, thus reducing its fat content to one-quarter of that of traditional pesto.

INGREDIENTS

8 oz/225 g dried spaghetti or linguine

fresh basil sprigs, to garnish

LOWFAT PESTO

2 oz/55 g fresh basil leaves

1 oz/25 g fresh flatleaf parsley sprigs

1 garlic clove, coarsely chopped

¼ cup pine nuts

½ cup lowfat curd cheese

¾ oz/20 g Parmesan cheese

salt and pepper

variation

You could substitute pecorino—Italian ewe's milk cheese—for the Parmesan cheese, if you like.

cook's tip

If the pesto is too thick, you can dilute it with a little of the pasta cooking water, but remember to reserve the water when you drain the pasta.

1 Bring a large pan of lightly salted water to a boil over medium heat. Add the pasta, return to a boil and cook for 8–10 minutes, or until tender but still firm to the bite.

2 Meanwhile, make the pesto. Put half the basil, half the parsley, the garlic, pine nuts, and curd cheese into a food processor and process until smooth. Add the remaining basil and parsley, then grate and add the Parmesan cheese. Season to taste with salt and pepper. Process again briefly.

3 Drain the cooked pasta and return to the pan. Add the pesto to the pasta and toss thoroughly with 2 forks.

Transfer to 4 large, warmed serving plates, garnish with a few sprigs of fresh basil and serve immediately.

fettuccine with smoked salmon

serves 4   **prep: 5 mins** ⟳   **cook: 10 mins** ⟳

This simple dish takes just moments to make, looks lovely, tastes fabulous and contains absolutely no saturated fat—what more could you possibly want?

INGREDIENTS

salt and pepper	2 oz/55 g smoked salmon,
8 oz/225 g dried fettuccine	cut into thin strips
1 tsp olive oil	1¼ cups watercress leaves,
1 garlic clove, finely chopped	plus extra to garnish

NUTRITIONAL INFORMATION

Calories	.222
Protein	.11g
Carbohydrate	.42g
Sugars	.2g
Fat	.3g
Saturates	.0g

variation

Substitute the same amount of arugula for the watercress, if you like, and garnish with a few sprigs of fresh flatleaf parsley.

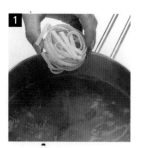

cook's tip

You can often buy misshapen offcuts of smoked salmon for a fraction of the price of neat smoked salmon slices in some large supermarkets.

1 Bring a large pan of lightly salted water to a boil over medium heat. Add the pasta, return to a boil and cook for 8–10 minutes, or until tender but still firm to the bite.

2 Meanwhile, heat the olive oil in a large nonstick skillet. Add the garlic and cook over low heat, stirring constantly, for 30 seconds. Add the salmon and watercress, season to taste with pepper, and cook for an additional 30 seconds, or until the watercress has wilted.

3 Drain the cooked pasta and return to the pan. Mix the salmon and watercress with the pasta. Toss the mixture thoroughly using 2 large forks. Divide between 4 large serving plates and garnish with extra watercress leaves. Serve immediately.

scrumptious sandwiches

serves 1   prep: 5 mins   cook: 0 mins

Use your favorite type of bread or rolls, such as sourdough or rye, for these delicious sandwich fillings.

INGREDIENTS

2 slices bread or 1 roll

TUNA AND WATERCRESS FILLING

2 tbsp canned tuna in brine, drained

2 tbsp finely chopped watercress

1 tbsp canned corn, drained

2 tbsp Mayonnaise (see page 12)

½ tsp Dijon mustard

dash of lemon juice

salt and pepper

SHRIMP AND COTTAGE CHEESE FILLING

2 tbsp lowfat cottage cheese

¼ tsp tomato paste

pepper

6 cooked shelled shrimp

1 button mushroom, thinly sliced

2–3 slices red bell pepper

1 fresh chive, snipped

CHICKEN FILLING

1 tbsp fat free cream cheese

1–2 romaine lettuce leaves, shredded

25 g/1 oz cooked chicken, skinned and cut into thin strips

¼ tsp Dijon mustard

½ celery stalk, sliced

3 shelled pistachio nuts, sliced

salt and pepper

NUTRITIONAL INFORMATION

Calories	.296/250/260
Protein	.22/22/19g
Carbohydrate	.42/35/36g
Sugars	.6/5/6g
Fat	.6/3/5g
Saturates	.2/1/1g

variation

Following the tuna recipe, replace the fish with crabmeat, the watercress with arugula and the mustard with 1 teaspoon finely chopped chile.

cook's tip

If you are not going to eat the sandwich immediately, wrap it loosely in plastic wrap or waxed paper and store in the refrigerator.

1 To make the tuna and watercress filling, put all the ingredients in a large mixing bowl and, using a metal spoon, stir until thoroughly blended. Spread the tuna mixture evenly over 1 slice of bread or half a roll, then season to taste with salt and pepper and top with the remaining slice or half roll. Serve immediately.

2 To make the shrimp and cottage cheese filling, place the cottage cheese in a small bowl, stir in the tomato paste and season to taste with pepper. Spread the cheese mixture over 1 slice of bread or half a roll and top with the cooked shrimp and slices of mushroom and bell pepper. Sprinkle with the snipped chive and top with the remaining

slice of bread or half roll. Serve immediately.

3 To make the chicken filling, spread the cream cheese over 1 slice of bread or half a roll and place the lettuce on top. Toss the chicken with the mustard in a small bowl and arrange over the lettuce, then top with the celery and nuts and season

to taste with salt and pepper. Top with the remaining slice of bread or half roll.

sausage & lentil stew

serves 4   prep: 5 mins ⟲   cook: 1 hr

This warming one-pot meal is perfect for an easy light supper. Like all sausages, Spanish chorizo is high in fat, but it is so flavorsome that you require only a small quantity to liven up the lentils.

INGREDIENTS

2 oz/55 g chorizo sausage,
very thinly sliced
1 onion, finely chopped
1⅓ cups Puy lentils
2½ cups Chicken Stock
(see page 11)
1¾ cups water
1 carrot, thinly sliced
1 celery stalk, thinly sliced
2 tsp chopped fresh parsley
salt and pepper

NUTRITIONAL INFORMATION

Calories	.217
Protein	.17g
Carbohydrate	.30g
Sugars	.3g
Fat	.4g
Saturates	.1g

cook's tip

Puy lentils are best for this stew, as they have a fine flavor and hold their shape well when cooked. You could use brown lentils instead, but split red ones would become too mushy.

1 Set aside a few slices of chorizo for the garnish and cut the remaining slices into thin strips. Dry-fry the slices and strips in a skillet over low heat, stirring frequently, for 2–3 minutes. Remove the chorizo slices and set aside. Add the onion to the skillet and cook, stirring occasionally, for an additional 5 minutes, or until softened.

2 Transfer the onion to a heavy-bottom pan. Add the lentils, Chicken Stock, and water and bring to a boil over medium heat. Cover and let simmer for 30–40 minutes, or until the lentils are tender.

3 Add the carrot, celery, and parsley and season to taste with salt and pepper. Cover and let simmer for an additional 8–10 minutes, or until the carrot is tender. Serve immediately, garnished with the reserved chorizo slices.

sweet & sour drumsticks

cook: 20 mins   **prep: 15 mins, plus 1 hr marinating**   **serves 4**

Chicken drumsticks are marinated to impart a tangy, sweet and sour flavor and a shiny glaze before being cooked on a barbecue. They are ideal served as part of an alfresco summer party.

NUTRITIONAL INFORMATION	
Calories 171	
Protein 33g	
Carbohydrate 10g	
Sugars 9g	
Fat 5g	
Saturates 1g	

INGREDIENTS

8 chicken drumsticks

4 tbsp red wine vinegar

2 tbsp tomato paste

2 tbsp soy sauce

2 tbsp honey

1 tbsp Worcestershire sauce

1 garlic clove, finely chopped

good pinch of cayenne pepper

salt and pepper

crisp salad greens, to serve

cook's tip

For a tangy flavor, add the juice of 1 lime to the marinade. While the drumsticks are broiling, check regularly to ensure that they are not burning.

1 Skin the chicken drumsticks, if you like and slash 2–3 times with a sharp knife. Arrange the drumsticks in a single layer in a large, nonmetallic shallow dish.

2 Mix the vinegar, tomato paste, soy sauce, honey, Worcestershire sauce, and garlic together in a small bowl.

Season to taste with cayenne, salt and pepper, then pour the mixture over the drumsticks, turning to coat thoroughly in the marinade.

3 Cover with plastic wrap and let marinate in the refrigerator for 1 hour. Preheat the broiler to high or light a barbecue. Line a broiler rack with foil and place the

drumsticks on top. Cook under the broiler or over hot coals for 20 minutes, brushing with the marinade during cooking, until the chicken is well browned and the juices run clear when pierced with a tip of a knife.

4 Transfer the drumsticks to a warmed serving dish and serve immediately with crisp salad greens.

spicy chicken with naan

serves 4   **prep: 10 mins,**   **cook: 20 mins**
                   plus 1–2 hrs marinating

This easy Indian-style dish makes a delicious lunch or supper and can be served with additional salad, if you like. It is also excellent served cold. Make mini chicken naan for children's lunch boxes.

INGREDIENTS

1 lb/450 g skinless, boneless chicken, trimmed of all visible fat and cut into ½-inch/2.5-cm cubes

4 naan breads

½ onion, sliced into rings

2 tomatoes, thinly sliced

¼ iceberg lettuce, shredded

MARINADE

3 tbsp lowfat plain yogurt

1 tsp garam masala

1 tsp chili powder

2 tbsp lime juice

2 tbsp chopped fresh cilantro

1 fresh red chile, seeded and finely chopped

salt and pepper

NUTRITIONAL INFORMATION	
Calories	503
Protein	42g
Carbohydrate	72g
Sugars	6g
Fat	15g
Saturates	3g

variation

You could serve the chicken and salad in pita pockets, if you like. Toast the pita breads lightly first, then cut a slit with a sharp knife to make a pocket.

cook's tip

To make the chicken less spicy, use just ¼ teaspoon of garam masala and ¼ teaspoon of chili powder and omit the fresh chile in the marinade.

1 Place the chicken cubes in a shallow, nonmetallic dish. Put all the marinade ingredients in a measuring cup and stir until well blended, seasoning to taste with the salt and pepper. Pour the marinade over the chicken, tossing to coat well. Cover with plastic wrap and let marinate in the refrigerator for 1–2 hours.

2 Using a slotted spoon, transfer the chicken to an ovenproof dish. Cook under a preheated hot broiler, stirring and turning occasionally, for 20 minutes, or until tender and cooked through.

3 Meanwhile, cut a slit in the naan breads to make a pocket. Fill the naan pockets with the cooked chicken, onion rings, tomato slices, and shredded lettuce and serve immediately.

minty lamb burgers

cook: 20 mins

prep: 15 mins,   **serves 4**
plus 1 hr 30 mins chilling

variation

If you have a limited amount of time, replace the dressing with store-bought tomato relish or mango chutney.

A delicious alternative to traditional hamburgers, these lowfat lamb burgers are flavored with chopped fresh mint and are accompanied with a smooth minty dressing.

INGREDIENTS

1½ cups lean ground lamb

1 medium onion, finely chopped

4 tbsp dry whole-wheat bread crumbs

2 tbsp mint jelly

salt and pepper

TO SERVE

4 whole-wheat baps, split

2 large tomatoes, sliced

small piece of cucumber, sliced

lettuce leaves

DRESSING

4 tbsp lowfat cream cheese

1 tbsp mint jelly, softened

2-inch/5-cm piece cucumber, finely diced

1 tbsp chopped fresh mint

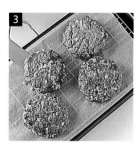

cook's tip

To cook on a preheated barbecue, place the burgers on a grill rack and cook for 8 minutes, turn over, and cook for 7 minutes, or until cooked through. Keep turning to stop them drying out and burning.

1 Place the lamb in a large bowl and mix in the onion, bread crumbs, and mint jelly. Season well with salt and pepper, then mold the ingredients together with your hands to form a firm mixture.

2 Divide the mixture into 4 portions and form each portion into a circle measuring 4 inches/10 cm

across. Place the circles on a plate lined with parchment paper and let chill in the refrigerator for 30 minutes.

3 Preheat the broiler to medium. Line a broiler rack with parchment paper, securing the ends under the rack, and place the burgers on top. Cook for 8 minutes, then turn the burgers over with a

spatula and cook for an additional 7 minutes, or until the burgers are cooked through.

4 Meanwhile, make the dressing. Mix the cream cheese, mint jelly, cucumber, and chopped mint together in a small bowl. Cover with plastic wrap and let chill in the refrigerator for 1 hour, or until

required. Drain the burgers on paper towels and serve inside baps with sliced tomatoes, cucumber, lettuce, and the dressing.

turkey patties

serves 4   **prep: 15 mins,** plus 30 mins chilling   **cook: 20–25 mins**

These savory patties are served with a colorful beet and apple sauce that gives a fabulous boost to the sometimes bland flavor of turkey. The sauce would taste just as good with plain broiled or griddled turkey breasts.

NUTRITIONAL INFORMATION

Calories	215
Protein	22g
Carbohydrate	26g
Sugars	10g
Fat	3g
Saturates	1g

INGREDIENTS

1½ tsp corn oil
1¼ cups spinach, shredded
2 garlic cloves, finely chopped
8 oz/225 g skinless, boneless turkey breast, trimmed of all visible fat and finely chopped
6 tbsp cold mashed potato
¾ cup lowfat cottage cheese, strained
3 scallions, chopped
1 tsp whole-grain mustard
2 tbsp chopped fresh basil
⅜ cup dried bread crumbs
salt and pepper
fresh dill sprigs, to garnish

SAUCE
1 peeled, cooked beet, finely diced
1 cup apple purée or unsweetened applesauce
1 tsp Dijon mustard
1 tsp snipped fresh dill

variation

If you are planning to cook the beet for the sauce yourself, you could use the green tops as a substitute for the spinach.

cook's tip

Dampen your hands slightly before forming the mixture into patties to prevent it from sticking to your fingers. To make it easier for coating, put the bread crumbs on a plate and roll the patties in them.

1 Preheat the oven to 375°F/190°C. To make the sauce, mix all the ingredients together in a bowl, cover with plastic wrap and let chill in the refrigerator until required. Alternatively, put all the ingredients in a food processor and process until smooth, then transfer to a small bowl, cover, and chill in the refrigerator until required.

2 To make the patties, heat the oil in a nonstick skillet. Add the spinach and garlic, then cover and cook over low heat for 2 minutes, or until the spinach has wilted. Remove from the heat and let cool. When cool, place in a bowl and mix with the turkey, potato, cottage cheese, scallions, mustard, basil, and half the bread crumbs. Season to taste with salt and pepper. Form the mixture into 8 patties, about ½-inch/1-cm thick. Coat with the remaining bread crumbs.

3 Place the patties on a baking sheet and bake in the preheated oven for 15–20 minutes, or until golden brown. Transfer to 4 warmed serving plates, add a spoonful of sauce to each plate and top with a fresh dill sprig. Serve immediately.

roast summer vegetables

serves 4   **prep: 10 mins** 🕐   **cook: 20–25 mins** ⏱

This appetizing and colorful mixture of Mediterranean vegetables makes a sensational summer lunch for vegetarians and meat-eaters alike. Roasting brings out the full flavor and sweetness of the bell peppers, eggplants, zucchinis, and onions.

INGREDIENTS

2 tbsp olive oil	1 orange bell pepper
1 fennel bulb	4 garlic cloves
2 red onions	4 fresh rosemary sprigs
2 beefsteak tomatoes	pepper
1 eggplant	crusty bread, to serve (optional)
2 zucchinis	
1 yellow bell pepper	
1 red bell pepper	

NUTRITIONAL INFORMATION

Calories	142
Protein	.4g
Carbohydrate	18g
Sugars	13g
Fat	.7g
Saturates	.1g

variation

Substitute a herb-flavored oil, such as tarragon or garlic and rosemary, for the plain olive oil, if you like.

cook's tip

You can also serve this dish as an accompaniment to broiled or grilled chicken or angler fish. This quantity will serve 8 people.

1 Preheat the oven to 400°F/200°C. Brush a large ovenproof dish with a little of the olive oil. Prepare the vegetables. Cut the fennel, red onions, and tomatoes into wedges. Slice the eggplant and zucchinis thickly, then seed all the bell peppers and cut into chunks. Arrange the vegetables in the dish and tuck the garlic cloves and rosemary sprigs between them. Drizzle with the remaining olive oil and season to taste with pepper.

2 Roast in the preheated oven for 10 minutes. Remove the dish from the oven and turn the vegetables over with a slotted spoon. Return to the oven and roast for an additional 10–15 minutes, or until all the vegetables are tender and starting to turn golden brown.

3 Serve the vegetables straight from the dish, or transfer to a warmed serving plate. Serve with crusty bread, if you like.

mexican eggs

serves 4 **prep: 10 mins** ⏲ **cook: 50 mins** ⏲

This dish is simple to prepare and makes the perfect lunch or light supper. Serve straight from the skillet with plenty of crisp salad greens or a selection of freshly steamed vegetables, if you like.

INGREDIENTS

1 tbsp corn oil
1 red bell pepper, seeded and cut into thin sticks
1 yellow bell pepper, seeded and cut into thin sticks
1 garlic clove, finely chopped
2 fresh red chiles, seeded and finely chopped
1 tsp ground coriander

1 tsp ground cumin
½ cup red wine
1 lb 12 oz/800 g canned chopped tomatoes
1 tsp brown sugar
salt and pepper
4 eggs
2 tbsp chopped fresh cilantro, to garnish

NUTRITIONAL INFORMATION	
Calories	156
Protein	8g
Carbohydrate	7g
Sugars	7g
Fat	8g
Saturates	2g

variation

If you like, omit the chiles and add 2 cups thinly sliced mushrooms and 8 oz/225 g canned corn with the tomatoes in Step 2.

cook's tip

Capsaicin—the substance that makes chiles hot—is not found in the seeds, but is concentrated in the flesh surrounding them. Removing the seeds will reduce the heat.

1 Heat the corn oil in a large skillet. Add the bell peppers and garlic and cook over medium heat, stirring occasionally, for 2 minutes, or until softened. Stir in the chiles, ground coriander, and cumin and cook for 1 minute. Pour in the red wine, bring to a boil, reduce the heat to medium, and let simmer for 3 minutes.

2 Stir in the tomatoes with their juice and the sugar, reduce the heat to low and let simmer gently for 20–25 minutes, or until thickened. Season to taste with salt and pepper.

3 Using a large spoon, make 4 hollows in the tomato mixture. Break an egg into each hollow, cover the skillet and cook for 10–15 minutes, or until set. Sprinkle with chopped fresh cilantro and serve.

soufflé omelet

serves 4   **prep: 15 mins** ⟳   **cook: 45 mins** ⟳

The combination of sweet cherry tomatoes, mixed mushrooms and peppery arugula leaves make a mouthwatering filling for these very light, fluffy omelets.

INGREDIENTS

6 oz/175 g cherry tomatoes

8 oz/225 g mixed mushrooms, such as white, shiitake, and oyster mushrooms

4 tbsp Vegetable Stock (see page 11)

small bunch of fresh thyme

salt and pepper

4 medium eggs, separated

8 tbsp water

4 medium egg whites

4 tsp olive oil

⅔ cup arugula leaves

fresh thyme sprigs, to garnish

NUTRITIONAL INFORMATION

Calories	146
Protein	10g
Carbohydrate	2g
Sugars	2g
Fat	11g
Saturates	2g

cook's tip

When whisking egg whites, make sure the bowl is spotlessly clean and free from grease, otherwise the egg whites will lose their shape.

1 Preheat the broiler to medium. Halve the tomatoes and place them in a large pan. Wipe the mushrooms with paper towels, trim if necessary and slice if large, then place them in the pan.

2 Add the Vegetable Stock and thyme to the pan. Bring to a boil, cover, and let simmer for 5–6 minutes, or until tender. Drain, remove and discard the thyme, and season to taste with salt and pepper. Keep warm.

3 Meanwhile, separate the eggs. Whisk the egg yolks with the water until frothy. Whisk the 8 egg whites in a spotlessly clean, grease-free bowl until stiff and dry.

4 Spoon the egg yolk mixture into the egg whites and, using a metal spoon, fold together until well mixed. Take care not to knock out too much of the air. Brush a small omelet pan with 1 teaspoon of olive oil and heat until hot. Pour in one-quarter of the egg mixture and cook for 4–5 minutes, or until the mixture has set. Finish cooking the omelet under the preheated hot broiler for 2–3 minutes. Transfer to a warmed serving plate and keep warm while cooking the remaining omelets. Fill the omelets with a few arugula leaves, and one-quarter of the mushroom mixture. Flip over the top, garnish with a few sprigs of thyme, and serve.

breakfast muffins

cook: 25 mins   prep: 20 mins   serves 4

Try this tasty and very filling breakfast or brunch—a lightly toasted whole-wheat English muffin, topped with lean bacon slices, broiled tomato, mushrooms, and a poached egg.

NUTRITIONAL INFORMATION	
Calories	159
Protein	12g
Carbohydrate	12g
Sugars	1g
Fat	7g
Saturates	20g

INGREDIENTS

2 whole-wheat English muffins

8 lean Canadian bacon slices, rinds removed

4 medium eggs

2 large tomatoes

salt and pepper

2 large flat mushrooms

4 tbsp Vegetable Stock (see page 11)

1 small bunch of fresh chives, snipped, to garnish

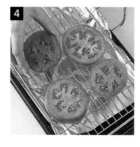

(see page 11)

variation

Omit the bacon for a vegetarian version and use more tomatoes and mushrooms. Alternatively, include a broiled lowfat tofu burger.

1 Preheat the broiler to medium. Cut the English muffins in half and lightly toast them under the hot broiler for 1–2 minutes on the open side. Transfer to a warmed plate and keep warm.

2 Trim off all visible fat from the bacon and cook under the preheated hot broiler for 2–3 minutes on each side, until cooked through. Drain on paper towels and keep warm.

3 Place 4 egg-poaching rings in a skillet, then pour in enough water to cover the bottom of the skillet. Bring to a boil and reduce the heat to a simmer. Break 1 egg into each ring and cook for 6 minutes, or until set.

4 Cut the tomatoes into 8 thick slices and arrange on foil on a broiler rack. Broil under the preheated hot broiler for 2–3 minutes, or until just cooked. Season to taste with salt and pepper. Peel and thickly slice the mushrooms. Place in a pan with the Vegetable Stock, bring to a boil, cover, and simmer for 4–5 minutes. Drain and keep warm. Arrange the tomato and mushroom slices on the toasted English muffins and top each with 2 bacon slices. Carefully place a poached egg on top of each and sprinkle with a little pepper. Garnish with snipped fresh chives and serve.

rice & tuna bell peppers

cook: 35 mins

prep: 10 mins

serves 4

Broiled mixed sweet bell peppers are filled with tender tuna, corn, nutty brown and wild rice, and grated, reduced-fat cheese. Serve with a large crisp salad to make a filling lunch.

variation

If you want to reduce the fat content in this dish further, then omit the Cheddar cheese and only use a little Parmesan cheese.

INGREDIENTS

generous ¼ cup wild rice

generous ¼ cup brown rice

4 assorted medium bell peppers

7 oz/200 g canned tuna in brine, drained and flaked

11½ oz/325 g canned corn kernels (with no added sugar or salt), drained

3½ oz/100 g reduced fat sharp Cheddar cheese, grated

1 bunch of fresh basil leaves, shredded

salt and pepper

2 tbsp dry white bread crumbs

1 tbsp freshly grated Parmesan cheese

fresh basil leaves, to garnish

crisp salad greens, to serve

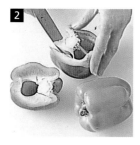

cook's tip

When cooking bell peppers under the broiler, make sure the broiler rack is lined with foil to catch any juices. Keep a close eye on them as they can burn.

1 Preheat the broiler to medium. Place the wild rice and brown rice in different pans, cover with water, and cook for 15 minutes, or according to the package instructions. Drain. Set aside.

2 Meanwhile, halve the bell peppers, remove the seeds and stalks and arrange the bell peppers on a broiler rack, cut-side down. Cook under the hot broiler for 5 minutes, turn over, and cook for 4–5 minutes.

3 Transfer the rice to a large bowl and add the tuna and corn. Gently fold in the grated cheese. Stir the basil leaves into the rice mixture, and season to taste with salt and pepper.

4 Divide the tuna and rice mixture into 8 equal portions, then pile each portion into each cooked bell pepper half. Mix the bread crumbs and Parmesan cheese together in a bowl and sprinkle over each bell pepper. Place the bell peppers under the preheated hot broiler and cook for 4–5 minutes, or until hot and golden brown. Transfer the bell peppers to a large serving plate, garnish with fresh basil leaves, and serve immediately with a crisp salad.

mushroom risotto

serves 4 **prep: 10 mins,** ⏱ **cook: 30 mins** ⏱
plus 30 mins soaking

To achieve the authentic creamy texture of risotto, use arborio or carnaroli rice. These shorter-grain varieties can absorb more liquid than long-grain rice, but still retain their "bite." They are widely available from supermarkets and may be labeled "risotto rice." Avoid easy-cook risotto rice, which will not have the same texture.

INGREDIENTS

1 tbsp dried porcini mushrooms

1¼ cups boiling water

1 tbsp olive oil

1 onion, finely chopped

1 garlic clove, finely chopped

1 fresh sage sprig, finely chopped

generous 1¼ cups risotto rice

½ cup white wine

8 oz/225 g cremini mushrooms, sliced

3 cups hot Vegetable Stock
(see page 11)

4 tbsp freshly grated Parmesan cheese

salt and pepper

shavings of fresh Parmesan cheese,
to garnish

NUTRITIONAL INFORMATION	
Calories	.384
Protein	.10g
Carbohydrate	.71g
Sugars	.2g
Fat	.7g
Saturates	.2g

variation

Instead of cremini mushrooms, use portobello mushrooms. Substitute Chicken Stock (see page 11) for Vegetable Stock, if you like.

cook's tip

Place the stock in a separate pan before you start cooking the risotto. Bring to a boil, then reduce the heat and let simmer to keep the stock at the right temperature while you add it to the rice.

1 Put the dried porcini mushrooms in a small bowl and pour in the boiling water to cover. Let soak for 30 minutes, or until the mushrooms are soft. Drain, reserving the soaking liquid. Using a sharp knife, chop the mushrooms and strain the soaking liquid through a coffee filter paper or cheesecloth-lined strainer.

2 Heat the olive oil in a large, heavy-bottom pan. Add the onion, garlic, and sage and cook, stirring frequently, for 5 minutes. Add the rice and cook over low heat, stirring constantly to coat the grains with the oil, for 3 minutes. Add the white wine and cook, stirring constantly, until it has evaporated. Stir in the porcini and cremini

mushrooms, the mushroom soaking liquid and a large ladleful of the hot Vegetable Stock. Let simmer, stirring constantly, until all the stock has been absorbed. Continue adding the Vegetable Stock and stirring in this way for 20 minutes, or until all the stock has been absorbed and the rice is tender but still firm to the bite.

3 Remove the pan from the heat, stir in the Parmesan cheese and season to taste with salt and pepper. Divide the risotto between 4 warmed serving plates, garnish with shavings of Parmesan cheese and serve.

cheesy ham savory

serves 4   **prep: 10 mins** ⏲   **cook: 7 mins** ⏲

Lean ham wrapped round crisp celery, topped with a light crust of cheese and scallions, makes a delicious light lunch. Serve with a fresh tomato salad and crusty bread.

INGREDIENTS

4 celery stalks

12 thin slices of lean ham

1 bunch of scallions

celery salt and pepper

¾ cup lowfat soft cheese with garlic and herbs

6 tbsp lowfat plain yogurt

4 tbsp freshly grated Parmesan cheese

TO SERVE

tomato salad

crusty bread

NUTRITIONAL INFORMATION

Calories	188
Protein	15g
Carbohydrate	5g
Sugars	5g
Fat	12g
Saturates	7g

cook's tip

Parmesan cheese is useful in lowfat recipes because its intense flavor means you need to use only a very small amount.

1 Preheat the broiler to medium. Wash the celery under cold running water, then remove any leaves and discard. Slice each celery stalk into 3 equal portions. Cut any visible fat off the ham and lay the slices on a cutting board. Place a portion of celery on each piece of ham and roll up. Place 3 rolls in each of 4 small, heatproof dishes.

2 Trim the scallions, then finely shred both the white and green parts. Sprinkle the scallions over the rolls and season to taste with celery salt and pepper.

3 Mix the soft cheese and yogurt together in a small bowl, then spoon the mixture over the rolls. Sprinkle each portion with 1 tablespoon of freshly grated Parmesan cheese and cook under the preheated hot broiler for 6–7 minutes, or until hot and the cheese has formed a crust. If the cheese starts to brown too quickly, reduce the temperature. Serve immediately with a tomato salad and crusty bread.

baked potatoes with pesto chicken

🕙 **cook: 1 hr–1 hr 15 mins**   🕙 **prep: 5 mins**   **serves 4**

*Filled baked potatoes make wonderful comfort food on a cold day,
but resist the urge to add butter, sour cream, or grated cheese. This
potato needs only a green salad to make a delicious light meal.*

NUTRITIONAL INFORMATION	
Calories 250	
Protein 20g	
Carbohydrate 31g	
Sugars 6g	
Fat 6g	
Saturates 1g	

INGREDIENTS

4 large potatoes

corn oil, for brushing

2 skinless, boneless chicken breasts,
about 4oz/115 g each, trimmed of
all visible fat

1 cup lowfat plain yogurt

1 tbsp lowfat Pesto (see page 58)

green salad, to serve

cook's tip

If you do not have a griddle
pan, cook the chicken under a
preheated hot broiler instead,
but leave the skin on to
prevent the flesh from drying
out. Remove the skin before
slicing the chicken.

1 Preheat the oven
to 400°F/200°C. Prick
the potatoes all over with a
fork and bake in the preheated
oven for 1–1¼ hours, or until
soft and cooked through.

2 About 15 minutes
before the potatoes are
ready, heat a grill pan and
brush with a little corn oil. Add
the chicken and cook over
medium–high heat for
5 minutes on each side, or
until cooked through and
tender. Meanwhile, put the
yogurt and pesto in a bowl
and mix until blended.

3 Slice the potatoes down
the center, almost right
through, and open out. Cut
the cooked chicken into slices.
Divide the slices between the
potatoes and top with the
yogurt. Transfer to 4 warmed
serving plates and serve with a
green salad.

potato & tuna quiche

⏱ **cook: 1 hr**   ⏱ **prep: 20 mins**   **serves 4**

variation

To make a vegetarian version, replace the tuna with 1 bunch of cooked asparagus spears arranged over the top. Proceed as in main recipe.

The base for this quiche is made from mashed potato instead of pastry, giving a softer textured shell for the tasty tuna filling.

INGREDIENTS

1 lb/450 g potatoes, peeled and diced	1¾ oz/50 g canned corn, drained
2 tbsp butter	⅔ cup skim milk
6 tbsp all-purpose flour, plus extra for dusting	3 eggs, beaten
	1 tbsp chopped fresh dill
	salt and pepper
FILLING	1¾ oz/50 g sharp lowfat Cheddar
1 tbsp vegetable oil	cheese, grated
1 shallot, chopped	fresh dill sprigs, to garnish
1 garlic clove, crushed	
1 red bell pepper, diced	TO SERVE
6 oz/175 g canned tuna in brine, drained	lemon wedges
	shredded celery

cook's tip

Place the tart pan on a large baking sheet before baking in the oven. This makes it much easier to handle and will also catch any drips.

1 Preheat the oven to 400°F/200°C. Cook the potatoes in a pan of boiling water for 10 minutes, or until tender.

2 Drain the potatoes and mash well. Add the butter and flour and mix to form a dough. Turn the dough out onto a lightly floured counter and knead, then press into an 8-inch/20-cm tart pan. Prick the base with a fork and line with parchment paper and dried beans. Bake blind in the preheated oven for 20 minutes.

3 Heat the vegetable oil in a skillet, add the shallot, garlic, and bell pepper and cook gently over low heat for 5 minutes. Drain well and spoon the mixture into the cooked tart shell. Flake the tuna and arrange it over the top with the corn.

4 Mix the milk and beaten eggs together in a bowl, then mix in the chopped dill. Season to taste with salt and pepper, then pour over the tuna and corn. Sprinkle over the grated cheese and bake in the preheated oven for 20 minutes, or until the filling has set. Garnish with fresh dill sprigs and serve with lemon wedges and shredded celery.

vegetable samosas

serves 4   **prep: 30 mins**   **cook: 35–40 mins**

Everyone will love these hot and spicy vegetable samosas as they are oven-baked rather than deep-fried. Serve either hot or cold with mango chutney as an appetizer or as part of a light lunch. They are also perfect as a snack at any time of the day.

INGREDIENTS

1 small potato, peeled and quartered
1 small carrot, halved
4 cauliflower florets
1 tsp corn oil, plus
extra for brushing
2 tsp lime juice
1 tbsp water
1 shallot, finely chopped
3 tbsp frozen peas
1 fresh green chile, seeded and
finely chopped
½ tsp cumin seeds

½ tsp black cumin seeds
½ tsp ground turmeric
½ tsp ground coriander
beaten egg, to glaze
mango chutney, to serve

PASTRY
⅜ cup malted flour
1⅛ cups all-purpose flour, plus extra
for dusting
⅜ cup sunflower margarine
¼ cup skim milk

NUTRITIONAL INFORMATION

Calories	139
Protein	. . . . .4g
Carbohydrate	. . . . .19g
Sugars	. . . . .2g
Fat	. . . . .6g
Saturates	. . . . .2g

variation

If you would like these samosas to taste a little spicier, use 2 fresh green chiles, seeded and finely chopped, instead of just one.

cook's tip

If you have time, wrap the dough in foil and let chill in the refrigerator for 15–30 minutes before you roll it out.

1 Preheat the oven to 375°F/190°C. Cook the potato, carrot, and cauliflower in a small pan of boiling water for 10 minutes. Drain, let cool slightly, then chop. Put the oil, lime juice, water, shallot, peas, chile, and spices in a small pan, bring to a boil, then reduce the heat and let simmer gently, stirring occasionally, for 3 minutes.

Stir in the potato, carrot, and cauliflower and transfer to a bowl to cool.

2 To make the pastry, sift the flours into a bowl, add the margarine and rub in with your fingertips until the mixture resembles bread crumbs. Add just enough milk to make a firm dough. Turn out onto a lightly floured

counter and knead gently until smooth. Divide the dough into 4 equal pieces and roll each out into an 7-inch/18-cm circle. Trim the edges and cut each circle in half.

3 Brush a baking sheet with a little corn oil. Divide the vegetable mixture between the dough semicircles, placing it on one

half only and leaving a small border. Brush the edges with water, fold the dough over, and seal, pressing the edges together. Brush with beaten egg, transfer to the baking sheet and bake in the oven for 20–25 minutes, or until golden brown. Serve hot or cold with mango chutney.

layered vegetable bake

serves 4   **prep: 10 mins** ⏲   **cook: 1 hr 30 mins** ⏲

Simplicity to prepare, this tasty bake makes a superb meal in itself or can be served as a vegetable accompaniment to griddled chicken, in which case it will serve 8 people.

INGREDIENTS

1 tbsp olive oil, for brushing

1 lb 8 oz/675 g potatoes

2 leeks

2 beefsteak tomatoes

8 fresh basil leaves

1 garlic clove, finely chopped

1¼ cups Vegetable Stock

(see page 11)

salt and pepper

NUTRITIONAL INFORMATION

Calories 174

Protein 5g

Carbohydrate 33g

Sugars 4g

Fat 4g

Saturates 1g

variation

You could add 2 thinly sliced zucchinis to the layers of leeks for an even more substantial supper dish.

1 Preheat the oven to 350°F/180°C. Brush a large ovenproof dish with a little of the olive oil. Prepare all the vegetables. Peel and thinly slice the potatoes, trim and thinly slice the leeks, and slice the tomatoes. Place a layer of potato slices in the bottom of the dish, sprinkle with half of the basil leaves and cover with a layer of leeks. Top with a

layer of tomato slices. Repeat these layers until all the vegetables are used up, ending with a layer of potatoes.

2 Stir the chopped garlic into the Vegetable Stock and season to taste with salt and pepper. Pour the stock over the vegetables and brush the top with the remaining olive oil.

3 Bake in the preheated oven for 1½ hours, or until the vegetables are tender and the topping is golden brown. Serve immediately.

cottage potatoes

⏱ **cook: 1 hr**　　　　　　⏱ **prep: 10 mins**　　　　　　**serves 4**

Give the humble potato a surprising kick with this delicious spiced cheese filling. Serve with a tomato and onion salad or on a bed of colorful mixed salad greens.

NUTRITIONAL INFORMATION	
Calories	211
Protein	. . . . .11g
Carbohydrate	. . . . .29g
Sugars	. . . . .3g
Fat	. . . . .6g
Saturates	. . . . .1g

INGREDIENTS

4 baking potatoes

2 tsp sun-dried tomato paste

½ tsp ground coriander

salt and pepper

1 tbsp olive oil

3–4 scallions, finely chopped

1–2 fresh green chiles, seeded and finely chopped

1 tbsp tequila

1 tbsp finely chopped fresh cilantro

1 cup lowfat cottage cheese

fresh cilantro sprigs, to garnish

lime wedges, to serve

cook's tip

To cook the potatoes in the microwave, prick with a fork and put on paper towels. Cook on High for 6 minutes, turn over and cook for an additional 8 minutes.

1 Preheat the oven to 400°F/200°C. Cut a cross in the center of each potato and prick the skins with a fork. Wrap the potatoes individually in foil and bake for 1 hour, or until soft and cooked through.

2 Meanwhile, mix the sun-dried tomato paste and ground coriander together in a small bowl. Season to taste with salt and pepper. Just before the potatoes are ready, heat the olive oil in a small pan and add the scallions and chopped chiles. Cook, stirring occasionally, for 2–3 minutes, or until softened. Stir in the sun-dried tomato paste mixture and tequila and cook for an additional 1 minute. Remove from the heat and stir in the

chopped cilantro. Place the cottage cheese in a bowl and stir in the tomato mixture. Blend thoroughly.

3 Unwrap the potatoes and squeeze gently to open out the cut side. Divide the cottage cheese mixture equally between the potatoes and garnish with cilantro. Serve with lime wedges.

falafel

makes 24   **prep: 15 mins,** ⏱   **cook: 2 hrs** 🍳
plus 1 hr chilling

These scrumptious Middle Eastern morsels are a must-have on a buffet table and are ideal snacks for any time of day. Traditionally they are deep-fried, but here they are oven-baked and served with a spicy yogurt dip to counteract the slightly drier texture.

INGREDIENTS

1 cup dried chickpeas, soaked
overnight and drained
1 onion, chopped
2 garlic cloves, chopped
2 tsp cumin seeds
2 tsp ground coriander
2 tbsp chopped fresh parsley
2 tbsp chopped fresh cilantro
salt and pepper
corn oil, for brushing

DIP
½ cup lowfat plain yogurt
1 tbsp chopped fresh cilantro
1 tbsp chopped fresh mint
2 tsp grated onion
1 fresh red chile, seeded and
finely chopped
¼ tsp ground cumin
dash of lemon juice

NUTRITIONAL INFORMATION	
Calories	.42
Protein	.3g
Carbohydrate	.6g
Sugars	.1g
Fat	.1g
Saturates	.0g

variation

If time is limited use 8 oz/225 g canned chickpeas instead of dried. Replace the yogurt with fat free mascarpone cheese for a thicker dip.

cook's tip

When cooking dried chickpeas, skim off any scum that rises to the surface during cooking with a slotted spoon and always season after they have been cooked, otherwise they will become tough.

1 Put the chickpeas in a pan, cover with water, and bring to a boil over medium heat. Cook for 1–1½ hours, or until tender, then drain. Put the chickpeas, onion, garlic, cumin seeds, ground coriander, parsley, and fresh cilantro in a food processor and process until a firm paste forms. Transfer to a bowl, season to taste with salt and pepper, cover with plastic wrap, and let chill in the refrigerator for 1 hour.

2 To make the dip, mix all the ingredients together in a bowl, cover, and let chill in the refrigerator until required.

3 Preheat the oven to 400°F/200°C. Brush a baking sheet with corn oil.

Using your hands, form the chickpea mixture into walnut-size balls, place on the prepared baking sheet and flatten them slightly. Brush with corn oil and bake in the oven for 15 minutes. Turn over and bake for an additional 15 minutes, or until brown. Serve warm, with the yogurt dip.

poor man's tomatoes

serves 4   **prep: 20 mins**   **cook: 35 mins**

These elegantly filled tomatoes are perfect for any occasion, whether they are used for a family supper or as an appetizer for a dinner party. They are ideal served with a fresh, crisp salad.

INGREDIENTS

4 large tomatoes

2 tbsp finely chopped fresh basil

4 tsp olive oil

10 oz/280 g white mushrooms, very finely chopped

1 small onion, very finely chopped

2 garlic cloves, very finely chopped

1 tablespoon chopped fresh parsley

salt and pepper

1 cup Vegetable Stock (see page 11)

1 tbsp freshly grated Parmesan cheese

fresh basil sprigs, to garnish

NUTRITIONAL INFORMATION

Calories 78

Protein 3g

Carbohydrate 6g

Sugars 6g

Fat 5g

Saturates 1g

variation

To fill bell peppers, cut the tops off and seed. Blanch in boiling water for 2 minutes. Drain. Make the filling with 4 tomatoes.

1 Preheat the oven to 350°F/180°C. Slice a "lid" from the top of each tomato and set aside. Using a teaspoon, carefully scoop out the flesh from the tomato shells and chop. Place it in a small bowl and add 1 teaspoon of the chopped fresh basil. Invert the tomato shells onto paper towels and let drain.

2 Heat 3 teaspoons of the olive oil in a skillet. Add the mushrooms, onion, garlic, parsley, and remaining basil, then season to taste with pepper. Cover and cook over low heat for 2 minutes, then remove the lid and cook, stirring occasionally, for an additional 8–10 minutes. Meanwhile, bring the stock to a boil and cook until reduced

by three-quarters. Stir in the tomato mixture and cook for an additional 3–4 minutes, or until thickened. Press the mixture through a strainer with a wooden spoon and stir it into the mushroom mixture. Stir in the Parmesan cheese.

3 Stand the tomatoes, the right way up, in an ovenproof dish and season the

insides with salt. Divide the filling mixture between them and replace the "lids." Brush with the remaining olive oil and bake in the preheated oven for 15 minutes, or until tender and cooked through. Garnish with a few sprigs of fresh basil and serve warm.

corn & bell pepper crêpes

cook: 20 mins   **prep: 15 mins**   serves 4

These light-as-air crêpes are very appealing, so it's fortunate that they are so easy to make. For best results, use a heavy-bottom skillet or grill pan, preferably one with a nonstick lining.

NUTRITIONAL INFORMATION
Calories 239
Protein 8g
Carbohydrate 40g
Sugars 3g
Fat 6g
Saturates 1g

INGREDIENTS

⅓ cup frozen corn
kernels, thawed
4 tbsp cornmeal
4 tbsp all-purpose flour
1 small red bell pepper, seeded and
very finely chopped
1 small egg yolk
½ tsp superfine sugar
2 egg whites
1 tbsp olive oil

variation

You can use the same quantity of fresh corn as canned, in which case, you will require 1 large cob.

1 Put half the corn kernels in a food processor and process until finely chopped. Place the remaining corn kernels, cornmeal, flour, and chopped bell pepper in a bowl and add the processed corn. Beat the egg yolk with the sugar in a separate small bowl, then add it to the corn mixture and stir thoroughly.

2 Beat the egg whites in a spotlessly clean, greasefree bowl until they stand in soft peaks. Gently fold half the egg whites into the corn mixture, then fold in the remaining egg whites.

3 Heat half the olive oil in a heavy-bottom skillet. Drop spoonfuls of the batter into the skillet, spacing them well apart, and cook for 3 minutes, or until the undersides are golden brown. Flip over carefully with a spatula and cook the other sides for 3 minutes, or until golden brown. Transfer to a warmed serving plate and keep warm while you cook the remaining crêpes, adding more oil, if necessary. Serve immediately.

pasta niçoise salad

serves 4 **prep: 15 mins** ⟲ **cook: 35 mins** ⟳

Based on the classic French salad niçoise, this recipe has a light olive oil dressing with the tang of capers and the fragrance of fresh basil.

INGREDIENTS

8 oz/225 g dried farfalle

salt and pepper

6 oz/175 g green beans, stems and heads removed

12 oz/350 g fresh tuna steaks

4 oz/115 g baby plum tomatoes, halved

8 anchovy fillets, drained on paper towels

2 tbsp capers in brine, drained

2 tbsp pitted black olives in brine, drained

fresh basil leaves, to garnish

DRESSING

1 tbsp olive oil

1 garlic clove, crushed

1 tbsp lemon juice

½ tsp finely grated lemon rind

1 tbsp shredded fresh basil leaves

NUTRITIONAL INFORMATION	
Calories	.214
Protein	.26g
Carbohydrate	.14g
Sugars	.2g
Fat	.7g
Saturates	.1g

variation

Any pasta shape is suitable for this salad—to make it even more colorful, use tricolor pasta.

cook's tip

Dried pasta will keep for 6 months. Once opened, the package should be resealed or the pasta should be kept in an airtight jar.

1 Preheat the broiler to medium. Cook the pasta in a large, heavy-bottom pan of lightly salted boiling water according to the package instructions, or until just tender but still firm to the bite. Drain, return to the pan, and keep warm.

2 Cook the green beans in a small pan of lightly salted boiling water for 5–6 minutes, or until just tender. Drain well and toss into the pasta. Keep warm.

3 Rinse the tuna under cold running water and pat dry on paper towels. Season on both sides with pepper. Place the tuna on a broiler rack and cook for 4–5 minutes on each side, or until cooked through. Drain the tuna on paper towels and, using a knife and fork, flake into bite-size pieces. Toss the tuna into the pasta together with the tomatoes, anchovies, capers, and olives. Set aside and keep warm.

4 Meanwhile, prepare the dressing. Mix all the ingredients together in a small bowl and season well with salt and pepper. Pour the dressing over the pasta mixture and mix carefully. Transfer to a warmed serving bowl and garnish with fresh basil leaves. Serve.

mackerel & potato salad

serves 4   **prep: 25 mins,** ⏱ **plus 6 hrs chilling**   **cook: 10 mins** ⏱

Inexpensive and packed with flavor, mackerel is an ideal fish to use in salads. In this recipe, it is combined with nutty new potatoes, apple, arugula, and cucumber.

INGREDIENTS

4½ oz/125 g new potatoes, scrubbed and diced

8 oz/225 g mackerel fillets, skinned

5 cups water

1 bay leaf

1 slice of lemon

1 eating apple, cored and diced

1 shallot, thinly sliced

3 tbsp white wine vinegar

1 tsp corn oil

1½ tsp superfine sugar

¼ tsp Dijon mustard

salt and pepper

TO SERVE

2 tbsp lowfat plain yogurt

¼ cucumber, thinly sliced

1 tbsp snipped fresh chives

1 bunch of arugula

NUTRITIONAL INFORMATION

Calories 182

Protein 12g

Carbohydrate 11g

Sugars 6g

Fat 10g

Saturates 2g

variation

Fresh salmon is very versatile and would work equally well in this dish. Replace the mackerel fillets with the same quantity of salmon fillets.

cook's tip

If new potatoes are not in season, use a waxy, firm-fleshed potato, such as round red, round white, or All Blue potatoes instead.

1 Steam the potatoes over a pan of simmering water for 10 minutes, or until tender. Meanwhile, using a sharp knife, remove the skin from the mackerel fillets and cut into bite-size pieces. Bring the water to a boil in a large, shallow pan, then reduce the heat so that it is just simmering and add the mackerel pieces, bay leaf, and lemon. Poach for 3 minutes, or until the flesh is opaque. Remove the mackerel from the pan with a spatula and transfer to a serving dish.

2 Drain the potatoes well and transfer them to a large bowl. Mix with the apple and shallot, then spoon the mixture over the mackerel.

3 Mix the vinegar, oil sugar, and mustard together in a measuring cup, season to taste with salt and pepper and whisk well. Pour the dressing over the potato mixture. Cover and chill in the refrigerator for up to 6 hours.

4 To serve, spread the yogurt over the salad, then arrange the cucumber decoratively on top and sprinkle with the fresh chives. Surround the salad with the arugula.

thai potato crab cakes

serves 4 **prep: 10 mins** ⏲ **cook: 30 mins** ⏲

These small crab cakes are based on a traditional Thai recipe. They make a delicious snack any time of the day when served with this sweet and sour cucumber sauce.

INGREDIENTS

1 lb/450 g potatoes, peeled and diced

6 oz/175 g white crabmeat, drained if canned

4 scallions, chopped

1 tsp light soy sauce

½ tsp sesame oil

1 tsp chopped lemon grass

1 tsp lime juice

3 tbsp all-purpose flour, plus extra for dusting

salt and pepper

2 tbsp vegetable oil

SAUCE

4 tbsp finely chopped cucumber

2 tbsp honey

1 tbsp garlic wine vinegar

½ tsp light soy sauce

1 fresh red chile, seeded and chopped

TO GARNISH

1 fresh red chile, seeded and sliced

cucumber slices

NUTRITIONAL INFORMATION

Calories 254

Protein 12g

Carbohydrate 40g

Sugars 9g

Fat 6g

Saturates 1g

variation

If you like, replace the white crabmeat with canned tuna, drained and flaked, and the lime juice with lemon juice.

cook's tip

Fresh chiles can burn the skin several hours after chopping, so it is best to wear gloves when handling them. Alternatively, wash your hands thoroughly afterward.

1 Cook the diced potatoes in a large pan of boiling water for 10 minutes, or until cooked through. Drain well and mash.

2 Mix the crabmeat into the mashed potato with the scallions, soy sauce, sesame oil, lemon grass, lime juice, and flour. Season to taste with salt and pepper.

3 Divide the potato mixture into 8 equal-size portions and form them into small circles, using floured hands. Heat the vegetable oil in a preheated wok or large, heavy-bottom skillet and cook the cakes, 4 at a time, for 5–7 minutes, turning once. Transfer to a plate and keep warm. Repeat with the remaining crab cakes.

4 Meanwhile, make the sauce. Mix the cucumber, honey, vinegar, soy sauce, and chopped red chile together in a small bowl. Garnish the cakes with the sliced red chile and cucumber slices and serve immediately with the sauce.

cantaloupe & crab salad

serves 4   **prep: 15 mins** 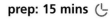   **cook: 0 mins**

This colorful salad combines delicious fresh crabmeat with flavorsome raw fruit and vegetables and a lowfat dressing— what could be healthier or more delicious?

INGREDIENTS

12 oz/350 g fresh crabmeat

5 tbsp Lowfat Mayonnaise
(see page 12)

¼ cup lowfat plain yogurt

4 tsp extra virgin olive oil

4 tsp lime juice

1 scallion, finely chopped

4 tsp finely chopped fresh parsley

pinch of cayenne pepper

1 cantaloupe melon

2 radicchio heads,
separated into leaves

fresh parsley sprigs, to garnish

NUTRITIONAL INFORMATION

Calories 252

Protein 20g

Carbohydrate 10g

Sugars 9g

Fat 15g

Saturates 1g

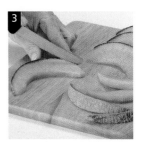

cook's tip

If fresh crabmeat is not available, you can use frozen crabmeat. Let the crab thaw thoroughly before making the salad.

1 Place the crabmeat in a large bowl and pick over it very carefully to remove any remaining shell or cartilage, but try not to break the meat up.

2 Put the lowfat Mayonnaise, yogurt, olive oil, lime juice, scallion, chopped fresh parsley, and cayenne pepper into a separate bowl and mix until thoroughly blended. Fold in the crabmeat.

3 Cut the melon in half and remove and discard the seeds. Thinly slice, then cut off the rind with a sharp knife.

4 Arrange the melon slices and radicchio leaves on 4 large serving plates, then arrange the crabmeat mixture on top. Garnish with a few sprigs of fresh parsley and serve.

thai noodle salad

🔥 cook: 3 mins   🕐 prep: 10 mins,
plus 30 mins soaking   serves 4

Thai salads are typically a contrasting mix of colors, textures, aromas, and flavors, and are designed to delight the eye as much as they tempt the taste buds.

NUTRITIONAL INFORMATION	
Calories	.272
Protein	.16g
Carbohydrate	.45g
Sugars	.6g
Fat	.3g
Saturates	.1g

INGREDIENTS

1 oz/25 g dried wood ears

2 oz/55 g dried Chinese mushrooms

4 oz/115 g cellophane noodles

½ cup cooked lean ground pork

4 oz/115 g shelled raw shrimp

5 fresh red chiles, seeded and
thinly sliced

1 tbsp chopped fresh cilantro

3 tbsp Thai fish sauce (nam pla)

3 tbsp lime juice

1 tbsp brown sugar

variation

For extra flavor, use the strained soaking water from the mushrooms—not the wood ears—for cooking the shrimp and the cooked ground pork.

1 Put the wood ears and Chinese mushrooms in separate bowls and pour over enough boiling water to cover. Let soak for 30 minutes. After 20 minutes, put the cellophane noodles in a separate bowl and pour over enough hot water to cover. Let the noodles soak for 10 minutes, or according to the package instructions.

2 Drain the wood ears, rinse thoroughly and cut into small pieces. Drain the mushrooms, squeezing out as much liquid as possible. Cut off and discard the stalks and cut the caps in half. Pour just enough water into a pan to cover the bottom and bring to a boil. Add the pork, shrimp, wood ears, and mushrooms and let simmer, stirring, for

3 minutes, or until cooked through. Drain well. Drain the noodles and cut them into short lengths with scissors.

3 Put the chiles, cilantro, fish sauce, lime juice, and brown sugar in a salad bowl and stir until the sugar has dissolved. Add the noodles and shrimp and pork mixture, toss well, and serve.

turkey & rice salad

serves 4   **prep: 15 mins,** ⟲ **plus 10 mins cooling**   **cook: 45 mins** ⟲

Rice salads are perfect at any time of year and are both economical and very easy to prepare. To enjoy the delicate flavor of this dish, serve it while it is still warm.

INGREDIENTS

4 cups Chicken Stock	**4 oz/115 g oyster mushrooms,**
(see page 11)	**torn into pieces**
scant 1 cup mixed long-grain	**¼ cup shelled pistachio nuts,**
and wild rice	**finely chopped**
2 tbsp corn oil	**2 tbsp chopped fresh cilantro**
8 oz/225 g skinless, boneless turkey	**1 tbsp snipped fresh garlic chives**
breast, trimmed of all visible fat and	**salt and pepper**
cut into thin strips	**1 tbsp balsamic vinegar**
2 cups snow peas	**fresh garlic chives, to garnish**

NUTRITIONAL INFORMATION

Calories	373
Protein	22g
Carbohydrate	40g
Sugars	2g
Fat	14g
Saturates	1g

variation

This salad would also look spectacular made with red rice. Cook as in the main recipe or follow the package instructions.

cook's tip

Before adding any of the ingredients to the preheated hot wok, swirl the corn oil gently and carefully so that it coats the sides as well as the bottom of the wok.

1 Set aside 3 tablespoons of the Chicken Stock and bring the remainder to a boil in a large pan. Add the rice and cook for 30 minutes, or until tender. Drain and let cool slightly.

2 Meanwhile, heat 1 tablespoon of the oil in a preheated wok or skillet. Stir-fry the turkey over medium heat for 3–4 minutes, or until cooked through. Using a slotted spoon, transfer the turkey to a dish. Add the snow peas and mushrooms to the wok and stir-fry for 1 minute. Add the reserved stock, bring to a boil, then reduce the heat, cover, and let simmer for 3–4 minutes. Transfer the vegetables to the dish and let cool slightly.

3 Thoroughly mix the rice, turkey, snow peas, mushrooms, nuts, cilantro, and garlic chives together, then season to taste with salt and pepper. Drizzle with the remaining corn oil and the vinegar and garnish with fresh garlic chives. Serve warm.

crêpes with curried crab

serves 4 **prep: 25 mins, plus 30 mins standing** **cook: 25 mins**

Homemade crêpes are delicious—here, white crabmeat is lightly flavored with curry spices and tossed in a lowfat dressing.

INGREDIENTS

scant ⅞ cup buckwheat flour

1 large egg, beaten

1¼ cups skim milk

4½ oz/125 g frozen spinach, thawed, well drained, and chopped

2 tsp vegetable oil

FILLING

12 oz/350 g white crabmeat

1 tsp mild curry powder

1 tbsp mango chutney

1 tbsp Lowfat Mayonnaise (see page 12)

2 tbsp lowfat plain yogurt

2 tbsp chopped fresh cilantro

TO SERVE

green salad

lemon wedges

NUTRITIONAL INFORMATION

Calories	.279
Protein	.25g
Carbohydrate	.31g
Sugars	.9g
Fat	.7g
Saturates	.1g

variation

If you like, try lean diced chicken in a light white sauce or shelled shrimp instead of the crab.

cook's tip

If you don't have a crêpe pan, then a small nonstick skillet would be suitable. Before adding the batter to the pan, stir or whisk it thoroughly to remove any lumps.

1 Sift the flour into a large bowl and remove and discard any husks that remain in the strainer. Make a well in the center of the flour and add the beaten egg. Using a balloon whisk, gradually whisk in the milk, then blend in the chopped spinach. Transfer the mixture to a large pitcher and let stand for 30 minutes.

2 To make the filling, mix all the ingredients together, except the cilantro, in a large bowl. Cover and let chill until required.

3 Whisk the batter. Brush a small crêpe pan with oil, then heat until hot. Pour in enough batter to cover the bottom thinly and cook for 1–2 minutes, then turn over and cook for 1 minute, or until golden. Transfer to a plate. Repeat to make 8 crêpes, layering them on the plate with parchment paper.

4 Stir the cilantro into the crab mixture. Fold each crêpe into quarters. Open one fold and fill with the crab mixture. Serve warm, with a salad and lemon wedges.

shrimp & rice salad

serves 4   **prep: 10 mins, plus 10 mins cooling**   **cook: 35 mins**

This colorful tropical salad is simplicity itself to prepare and tastes simply wonderful. For a special treat, you could use jumbo shrimp rather than their smaller Atlantic or Mediterranean cousins.

INGREDIENTS

scant 1 cup mixed long-grain and wild rice

salt and pepper

12 oz/350 g cooked shelled shrimp

1 mango, peeled, seeded, and diced

4 scallions, sliced

¼ cup slivered almonds

1 tbsp finely chopped fresh mint

DRESSING

1 tbsp extra virgin olive oil

2 tsp lime juice

1 garlic clove, crushed

1 tsp honey

salt and pepper

NUTRITIONAL INFORMATION

Calories 345

Protein 25g

Carbohydrate 43g

Sugars 8g

Fat 8g

Saturates 1g

---

variation

Substitute the same quantity of fresh or drained canned crabmeat for the shrimp, if you like.

cook's tip

If using jumbo shrimp for this dish instead of the ordinary ones, buy already cooked and shelled shrimp, which are available from most large supermarkets.

1 Cook the rice in a large pan of lightly salted boiling water for 35 minutes, or until tender. Drain and transfer to a large bowl, then add the shrimp.

2 To make the dressing, mix all the ingredients together in a large measuring cup, seasoning to taste with the salt and pepper, and whisk well until thoroughly blended. Pour the dressing over the rice and shrimp mixture and let cool.

3 Add the mango, scallions, almonds, and mint to the salad and season to taste with pepper. Stir thoroughly and transfer to a large serving dish and serve.

spicy chickpea snack

serves 4   **prep: 5 mins** ⏾   **cook: 10 mins** ⏱

You can use dried chickpeas, soaked overnight and cooked until soft, for this popular Indian snack, but the canned variety is just as flavorsome and works equally well.

INGREDIENTS

14 oz/400 g canned chickpeas, drained

2 medium potatoes, peeled

1 medium onion

2 tbsp tamarind paste

6 tbsp water

1 tsp chili powder

2 tsp sugar

salt and pepper

TO GARNISH

1 tomato, sliced

2 fresh green chiles, chopped

fresh cilantro leaves

NUTRITIONAL INFORMATION	
Calories	190
Protein	9g
Carbohydrate	34g
Sugars	4g
Fat	3g
Saturates	0.3g

cook's tip

Chickpeas have a nutty flavor and slightly crunchy texture. Indian cooks also grind these to make a flour called gram or besan, which is used to make breads and to thicken sauces.

1 Place the chickpeas in a small bowl and set aside until required.

2 Using a sharp knife, cut the potatoes into dice and cook in a large pan of boiling water for 7–8 minutes, or until cooked through. Drain the potatoes, return to the pan and set aside until required.

3 Using a sharp knife, finely chop the onion. Set aside until required.

4 Mix the tamarind paste and water together in a small bowl. Add the chili powder, sugar, and 1 teaspoon of salt and mix again. Pour the mixture over the chickpeas. Add the reserved onion and the diced potatoes, and stir to mix. Season to taste with salt and pepper. Transfer to a serving bowl and garnish with tomato slices, chiles, and fresh cilantro leaves.

potato & mushroom hash

🍳 **cook: 25–30 mins**　　　⏲ **prep: 10 mins**　　　**serves 4**

This is an easy one-pan dish, which is ideal for a very quick snack and packed with color and flavor. You can add any other type of vegetable you have at hand.

NUTRITIONAL INFORMATION	
Calories	378
Protein	18g
Carbohydrate	20g
Sugars	14g
Fat	26g
Saturates	7g

INGREDIENTS

1 lb 8 oz/675 g potatoes, peeled
and cubed

1 tbsp olive oil

2 garlic cloves, crushed

1 green bell pepper, seeded and cubed

1 yellow bell pepper, seeded and cubed

3 tomatoes, diced

2¾ oz/75 g white mushrooms, halved

1 tbsp Worcestershire sauce

2 tbsp chopped fresh basil

salt and pepper

fresh basil leaves, to garnish

cook's tip

Most brands of Worcestershire sauce contain anchovies. If cooking for vegetarians, make sure you use a vegetarian variety or omit it altogether.

1 Cook the potatoes in a large pan of boiling water for 7–8 minutes, or until tender. Drain well, return to the pan and set aside until required.

2 Heat the olive oil in a large, heavy-bottom skillet over medium heat. Add the potatoes and cook for 8–10 minutes, stirring constantly, until the potatoes are browned. Add the garlic and bell peppers to the skillet and cook for 2–3 minutes.

3 Stir in the tomatoes and mushrooms and cook, stirring constantly, for 5–6 minutes. Stir in the Worcestershire sauce and chopped basil, season to taste with salt and pepper, then transfer to a large serving dish. Garnish with a few fresh basil leaves and serve.

sweet potato & bean salad

serves 4   **prep: 10 mins** ⏱   **cook: 10 mins** ⏱

This piquant vegetarian salad is a meal in itself or can be served as an accompaniment to chicken or fish. Choose a mixture of colorful salad greens with a range of sweet and bitter flavors.

INGREDIENTS

1 sweet potato

4 baby carrots, halved

4 tomatoes

4 celery stalks, chopped

8 oz/225 g canned cranberry beans, drained and rinsed

4 oz/115 g mixed salad greens, such as frisée, arugula, radicchio and oak leaf lettuce

1 tbsp golden raisins

4 scallions, finely chopped

½ cup Honey and Yogurt Dressing (see Cook's Tip, page 12)

variation

Substitute your favorite beans for the cranberry beans—cannellini or flageolets would be equally good.

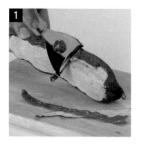

cook's tip

Cook the sweet potato in boiling water until it is just tender, otherwise it will absorb too much water and become unpleasantly soggy.

1 Peel and dice the sweet potato. Bring a pan of water to a boil over medium heat. Add the sweet potato and cook for 10 minutes, until tender. Drain the potato, transfer to a bowl, and set aside.

2 Cook the carrots in a separate pan of boiling water for 1 minute. Drain thoroughly and add to the sweet potato. Cut the tops off the tomatoes and scoop out the seeds. Chop the flesh and add to the bowl with the celery and beans. Mix well.

3 Line a large serving bowl with the mixed salad greens. Spoon the sweet potato and bean mixture on top, then sprinkle with the golden raisins and scallions. Spoon over the dressing and serve immediately.

main dishes

This chapter is the answer to that perennial question—what shall we have for supper tonight? Finding a solution can be a real headache when every cook book you turn to for good ideas seems packed with recipes notable for their heavy use of butter, cream, and other high-fat ingredients. Inspired by cuisines around the world, from Greece to China and from Morocco to Germany, these recipes feature marvelous main dishes based on meat, poultry, and vegetables. Many of them contain no more than ½ oz (15 g) fat per serving and some contain far less.

Stun sceptical guests with Stuffed Pork Fillet (see page 124), Roast Turkey with Cider Sauce (see page 150), or Moroccan Vegetable Stew (see page 154). No one will ever suggest again that lowfat cooking is boring and bland. Seduce the family into a healthier lifestyle with Swedish Lamb Stew (see page 138), Chicken with Saffron Mash (see page 140), or Vegetable & Tofu Stir-Fry (see page 152). Roasts, casseroles, stews, grills, and stir-fries are just some of the mouthwatering, healthy options that spoil you for choice. There is a dish for every season and all tastes, from subtle and creamy to warm and spicy. You will find quick and easy recipes for midweek suppers, succulent slow-cooked dishes for restful weekends, and gourmet delights for lowfat entertaining.

beef & broccoli in black bean sauce

serves 4　　　　**prep: 10 mins,** ☾　　　　**cook: 15 mins** ⏲
plus 6 hrs marinating

*Stir-fries are not only quick and easy to cook, but a healthy choice
as well. Because the cooking time is so brief, the vegetables retain
most of their nutrients—and their flavor and texture too.*

INGREDIENTS

8 oz/225 g lean rump steak

1 tbsp peanut or corn oil

8 oz/225 g broccoli, cut into florets

4 oz/115 g baby corn cobs,
cut in half diagonally

3 tbsp water

4 scallions, sliced diagonally

8 oz/225 g canned water chestnuts,
drained, rinsed, and sliced

MARINADE

1 tbsp fermented black beans, soaked
in cold water for 5–10 minutes

2 tbsp dark soy sauce

2 tbsp Chinese rice vinegar

1 tbsp peanut or corn oil

1 tsp brown sugar

1 garlic clove, thinly sliced

1 tbsp finely chopped fresh gingerroot

NUTRITIONAL INFORMATION

Calories 190

Protein 16g

Carbohydrate 12g

Sugars 3g

Fat 9g

Saturates 2g

variation

Use different combinations of
vegetables for this stir-fry, such as
zucchini strips, carrot sticks, bell
pepper strips, and cucumber sticks.

cook's tip

Fermented black beans are
available in cans or plastic
bags from Chinese food
stores. They should be soaked
in cold water before use to
remove any excess salt.

1 Using a sharp knife,
trim the steak of all
visible fat and thinly slice.
Put the steak in a large,
shallow, nonmetallic dish. To
make the marinade, mash the
black beans in a bowl with a
fork. Stir in the remaining
marinade ingredients until
thoroughly blended. Pour the
marinade over the steak,
turning to coat thoroughly.

Cover with plastic wrap and let
marinate in the refrigerator for
up to 6 hours.

2 Heat the peanut oil in a
preheated wok or large
skillet. Drain the steak and set
aside the marinade. Stir-fry the
steak over medium–high heat
for 3 minutes, then transfer to
a plate. Add the broccoli and
baby corn cobs to the wok and

stir in the water. Cover and
steam over low heat for
5 minutes, or until the
vegetables are tender.

3 Add the scallions and
water chestnuts to the
wok. Stir-fry for 2 minutes.
Return the steak to the wok
and pour in the reserved
marinade. Cook, stirring, until
heated through, then serve.

114　**low fat**

meatballs with tomato relish

serves 4　　　　**prep: 15 mins** ⏲　　　　**cook: 15–20 mins** ⏲

Even when ground beef is labeled "lean," it may contain more fat than we would like. It is best to buy a whole piece of lean beef, such as rump steak, trim off all visible fat and grind it yourself.

INGREDIENTS

1 onion, finely chopped

2 garlic cloves, finely chopped

2 slices bread, crusts removed

1 lb 2 oz/500 g lean beef, ground

1 cooked baby beet, chopped

pinch of paprika

2 tsp finely chopped fresh thyme

1 egg

salt and pepper

fresh thyme sprigs, to garnish

TOMATO RELISH

⅔ cup strained tomatoes

2 tsp creamed horseradish

NUTRITIONAL INFORMATION

Calories	243
Protein	30g
Carbohydrate	14g
Sugars	5g
Fat	8g
Saturates	3g

cook's tip

It is easy to cook beet yourself. Clean them and trim the stalks, then cook in a pan of simmering lightly salted water for 1–2 hours until tender. Drain and let cool, then peel.

1 Preheat the oven to 450°F/230°C. To make the tomato relish, mix the strained tomatoes and creamed horseradish together in a small bowl. Cover and set aside until required.

2 Put the onion, garlic, and 2 teaspoons of water in a small pan and let simmer over low heat for 5 minutes. Increase the heat, bring to a boil and cook until all the water has evaporated. Remove from the heat.

3 Meanwhile, tear the bread into pieces and place in a small bowl. Add enough cold water just to cover and let soak for 5 minutes. Squeeze the excess water from the bread and place in a bowl with the ground beef, onion and garlic mixture, beet, paprika, thyme, and egg. Season to taste with salt and pepper and mix thoroughly.

4 Form the mixture into 24 small balls between the palms of your hands. Thread 3 balls onto each of 8 metal skewers and place on a baking sheet. Bake in the preheated oven for 10 minutes, or until well browned. Transfer to a serving dish, garnish with a few sprigs of fresh thyme and serve with the tomato relish.

beef in beer

cook: 2 hrs–2 hrs 30 mins   **prep: 15 mins**   **serves 4**

Beef and beer is a traditional combination in all brewing countries, especially in Belgium, Germany, and Ireland. Use a strong dark beer or stout to create the fullest flavor.

NUTRITIONAL INFORMATION

Calories	.224
Protein	.27g
Carbohydrate	.6g
Sugars	.5g
Fat	.9g
Saturates	.3g

INGREDIENTS

few sprigs of fresh parsley

1 tbsp corn oil

1 lb 2 oz/500 g lean stewing steak, trimmed of all visible fat and cut into 1-inch/2.5-cm cubes

1 onion, chopped

7 oz/200 g cremini mushrooms, cut in half

4 tsp dark brown sugar

1½ cups Beef Stock (see page 11)

1¼ cups dark beer or stout

salt and pepper

variation

You could add 1 thinly sliced carrot and 2 thinly sliced celery stalks halfway through cooking the mushrooms in Step 2.

1 Using a sharp knife, chop the fresh parsley finely and set aside until required. Heat the corn oil in a large, heavy-bottom skillet. Add the stewing steak and cook, stirring frequently, for 10 minutes, or until browned all over. Using a slotted spoon, transfer the meat to a large ovenproof casserole dish.

2 Add the onion to the skillet and cook over low heat, stirring occasionally, for 3 minutes. Add the mushrooms and sugar and cook, stirring occasionally, for 10 minutes. Transfer to the casserole with a slotted spoon.

3 Add the Beef Stock, beer, and reserved parsley to the casserole and season to taste with salt and pepper. Bring to a boil, cover, and let simmer over very low heat for 1½–2 hours, or until tender. Serve hot.

chili con carne

serves 4   prep: 5 mins ↻   cook: 2 hrs 30 mins ⏱

Probably the most popular Mexican dish and one that is a great favorite with everyone. The chili content can be increased to suit your taste. Serve with freshly cooked rice and tortillas, if you like.

INGREDIENTS

1 lb 10 oz/750 g lean braising or stewing steak	salt and pepper
2 tbsp vegetable oil	15 oz/425 g canned red kidney beans, drained and rinsed
1 large onion, sliced	½ teaspoon dried oregano
2–4 garlic cloves, crushed	1–2 tbsp chopped fresh parsley
1 tbsp all-purpose flour	chopped fresh herbs, to garnish
generous 1¾ cups tomato juice	
14 oz/400 g canned tomatoes	TO SERVE
1–2 tbsp sweet chili sauce	freshly cooked rice
1 tsp ground cumin	tortillas

NUTRITIONAL INFORMATION

Calories	.443
Protein	.48g
Carbohydrate	.30g
Sugars	.11g
Fat	.15g
Saturates	.4g

variation

For a vegetarian version, replace the beef with 5½ oz/150 g mycoprotein (Quorn™) or cooked brown lentils and adjust the cooking time.

cook's tip

Because chili con carne requires quite a lengthy cooking time, it saves time and fuel to prepare double the quantity you need and freeze half of it for another occasion. Thaw and use within 3–4 weeks.

1 Preheat the oven to 325°F/160°C. Using a sharp knife, cut the beef into ¾-inch/2-cm cubes. Heat the vegetable oil in a large flameproof casserole dish and cook the beef over medium heat until well sealed on all sides. Remove the beef from the casserole with a slotted spoon and set aside until required.

2 Add the onion and garlic to the casserole and cook until lightly browned; then stir in the flour and cook for 1–2 minutes.

3 Stir in the tomato juice and tomatoes and bring to a boil. Return the beef to the casserole and add the chili sauce, cumin, and salt and pepper to taste. Cover and cook in the preheated oven for 1½ hours, or until the beef is almost tender.

4 Stir in the kidney beans, oregano, and parsley, and adjust the seasoning to taste, if necessary. Cover the casserole and return to the oven for 45 minutes. Transfer to 4 large, warmed serving plates, sprinkle with chopped fresh herbs, and serve immediately with freshly cooked rice and tortillas.

rogan josh

cook: 1 hr 45 mins　　　　**prep: 10 mins**　　　　serves 6

NUTRITIONAL INFORMATION	
Calories	.248
Protein	.35g
Carbohydrate	.2g
Sugars	.2g
Fat	.11g
Saturates	.5g

variation

Replace the ghee with vegetable oil and if you like the dish less spicy, seed the chiles before using.

This is one of the best known curries. Rogan Josh means "red curry," and is so-called because of the red chiles in the recipe.

INGREDIENTS

2 tbsp ghee

2 lb 4 oz/1 kg lean braising steak, cut into 1-inch/2.5-cm cubes

1 onion, chopped finely

3 garlic cloves

1-inch/2.5-cm piece fresh gingerroot, grated

4 fresh red chiles, chopped

4 green cardamom pods

4 cloves

2 tsp coriander seeds

2 tsp cumin seeds

1 tsp paprika

1 tsp salt

1 bay leaf

½ cup lowfat plain yogurt

1-inch/2.5-cm piece cinnamon stick

⅔ cup hot water

pepper

¼ tsp garam masala

cook's tip

Use a spice mill, coffee grinder, or the more traditional mortar and pestle to grind spices. If using a coffee grinder, wash it thoroughly afterward.

1 Preheat the oven to 350°F/180°C. Heat the ghee in a large flameproof casserole and brown the steak cubes in batches. Remove the steak from the casserole and place in a bowl. Set aside until required.

2 Add the chopped onion to the casserole and cook for 3–4 minutes.

3 Place the garlic, ginger, chiles, cardamoms, cloves, coriander, cumin, paprika, and salt in a mortar, and using a pestle, grind to a paste. Add the spice paste and bay leaf to the casserole and stir until fragrant.

4 Return the meat and any juices in the bowl to the casserole and let simmer for 2–3 minutes. Gradually stir in the yogurt, keeping the sauce simmering. Add the cinnamon stick and stir in the water. Add pepper to taste.

5 Cover the casserole and cook in the preheated oven for 1¼ hours, or until the meat is very tender and the sauce is slightly reduced. Remove and discard the cinnamon stick and stir in the garam masala. Remove surplus oil from the surface of the casserole before serving.

sauerbraten

serves 4 **prep: 20 mins,** plus 48 hrs marinating **cook: 2 hrs 15 mins**

In this traditional German dish, long marinating makes the topside melt-in-the-mouth tender and imparts a marvelous spicy flavor. This dish makes the perfect treat for a special occasion.

INGREDIENTS

1 lb 10 oz/750 g top round of beef, trimmed of all visible fat
8 whole cloves
1 tbsp corn oil
1 cup Beef Stock (see page 11)
2 lb 4 oz/1 kg mixed root vegetables, such as carrots, potatoes, and rutabaga, peeled and cut into chunks
2 tbsp raisins
1½ tsp cornstarch
3 tbsp water
salt and pepper

MARINADE
¾ cup wine
5 tbsp red wine vinegar
1 onion, chopped
1½ tsp brown sugar
4 peppercorns
1 bay leaf
½ tsp ground allspice
½ tsp mustard

NUTRITIONAL INFORMATION

Calories	.445
Protein	.41g
Carbohydrate	.36g
Sugars	.25g
Fat	.12g
Saturates	.4g

variation

Try other root vegetables with this dish, such as chunks of parsnip, turnip, and celery root.

cook's tip

This rustic dish will taste superb if you serve it with a simple and traditional accompaniment of boiled potatoes or noodles.

1 To make the marinade, put all the ingredients, except the mustard, in a pan. Bring to simmering point, then remove from the heat and stir in the mustard. Stud the beef with cloves and place in a nonmetallic dish. Pour the marinade over, cover, and let cool, then let chill in the refrigerator for 2 days. About 1 hour before cooking, remove the beef, pat dry, and let stand at room temperature. Set aside the marinade.

2 Preheat the oven to 300°F/150°C. Heat the oil in an ovenproof casserole, add the beef, and cook over medium heat for 5–10 minutes, or until browned. Pour the marinade into the casserole through a strainer, add the stock, and bring to a boil. Cover and bake in the oven for 1 hour, turning and basting frequently with the cooking juices.

3 Meanwhile, blanch the vegetables in boiling water for 3 minutes, then drain. Arrange the vegetables round the beef, return to the oven, and cook for 1 hour, or until the beef is very tender and the vegetables are cooked.

4 Transfer the beef and vegetables to a serving dish. Place the casserole on low heat and add the raisins. Mix the cornstarch and water until smooth and stir into the cooking juices. Bring to a boil, stirring, then let simmer for 2–3 minutes. Season and serve.

stuffed pork fillet

serves 8   **prep: 25 mins, plus 6 hrs** ⌛ **chilling (optional)**   **cook: 1 hr 30 mins** 🍲

Dried fruit, such as prunes and apricots, balances the richness of pork superbly. This succulent pork fillet is perfect served hot for a family supper and would also be an excellent choice, served cold, for a buffet, summer party, or picnic.

INGREDIENTS

2 pork fillets, about 1 lb 2 oz/500 g each, trimmed of all visible fat

DRESSING

2 red onions, finely chopped

2 cups fresh whole-wheat bread crumbs

½ cup no-soak dried prunes, chopped

½ cup no-soak dried apricots, chopped

pinch of grated nutmeg

pinch of ground cinnamon

salt and pepper

1 egg white, lightly beaten

NUTRITIONAL INFORMATION	
Calories	265
Protein	29g
Carbohydrate	17g
Sugars	11g
Fat	9g
Saturates	3g

variation

For an elegant presentation, garnish the pork fillet with fresh arugula and serve, adding a few arugula leaves to each plate.

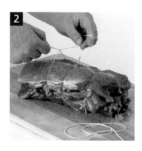

cook's tip

Dried fruit that does not need soaking is often labeled as "no-soak" fruit, and is available in the baking section of most large supermarkets.

1 Preheat the oven to 400°F/200°C. To make the dressing, mix the onions, bread crumbs, prunes, and apricots together. Season to taste with nutmeg, cinnamon, and salt and pepper. Stir in the egg white.

2 Cut a 5-inch/13-cm long piece from the narrow end of each pork fillet, then cut all the pieces almost completely in half lengthwise and open them out. Spread half the filling evenly over one of the longer pieces, then cover with both the smaller pieces, overlapping the narrow ends slightly. Spread the remaining filling on top and cover with the remaining piece of pork. Tie the pork loaf together with string or trussing thread at intervals along its length. Wrap it securely in foil and place in a roasting pan.

3 Cook the pork in the preheated oven for 1½ hours. If serving hot, let stand for 10 minutes before unwrapping, cutting off the string, and slicing. If serving cold, let cool in the wrapping, then let chill in the refrigerator for at least 2 hours and up to 6 hours before unwrapping and slicing.

stir-fried pork with snow peas

serves 4   **prep: 25 mins, plus ⏲ 40 mins standing/chilling**   **cook: 20 mins ⏱**

Served with rice or noodles, this substantial stir-fry makes a delicious midweek family supper. Prepare the garnish before you start cooking and serve with a flourish.

INGREDIENTS

8 dried Chinese mushrooms

1 lb/450 g pork fillet, trimmed of all visible fat and cut into thin strips

4 oz/115 g baby corn cobs

1 tbsp peanut or corn oil

1 garlic clove, finely chopped

1-inch/2.5-cm piece fresh gingerroot, cut into thin sticks

3½ cups snow peas

14 oz/400 g canned bamboo shoots, drained, rinsed, and thinly sliced

2 tsp dark soy sauce

2 tsp Chinese rice wine

4 tbsp Chicken or Vegetable Stock (see page 11)

2 tsp cornstarch

2 tbsp water

1 carrot, sliced into thin sticks

salt and pepper

1–2 scallions, trimmed, to garnish

MARINADE

1 tbsp dark soy sauce

1 tbsp Chinese rice wine

2 tsp cornstarch

pepper

NUTRITIONAL INFORMATION

Calories	.309
Protein	.31g
Carbohydrate	.22g
Sugars	.5g
Fat	.12g
Saturates	.3g

variation

You could add an extra, thinly sliced carrot and 2 thinly sliced celery stalks halfway through cooking the mushrooms in Step 4, if you like.

cook's tip

To rehydrate dried Chinese mushrooms, place the mushrooms in a small bowl and pour over enough hot water to cover. Let soak for 20 minutes.

1 To make the garnish, make a lengthwise cut 1-inch/2.5-cm long at one end of each scallion. Roll the onion through 90° and repeat. Repeat at the other end, then place in ice water to open out. Pat dry before using.

2 Rehydrate the Chinese mushrooms (see Cook's Tip). Mix all the marinade ingredients together in a nonmetallic dish, seasoning with the pepper. Add the pork, cover and let chill for 20 minutes. Blanch the corn in boiling water for 5 minutes. Drain and refresh in cold water.

3 Drain the mushrooms through a strainer, reserving the soaking water. Squeeze out any excess water, remove the stems, and slice the caps. Heat half the oil in a preheated wok, add the pork and stir-fry for 5 minutes, until browned. Set aside.

4 Wipe the wok, add the remaining oil and heat. Add the garlic and cook until golden. Remove with a slotted spoon and discard. Add the ginger, snow peas, bamboo shoots, and mushrooms, then stir-fry for 3 minutes. Stir in the soy sauce, wine, stock, and reserved soaking liquid. Cook for 2–3 minutes. Mix the cornstarch and water, add to the wok and stir until thickened. Return the pork and juices to the wok, add the corn and cook until heated through. Stir in the carrot, garnish with the scallions, and serve.

char shiu pork

serves 4　　　**prep: 20 mins, plus 2 hrs marinating**　　　**cook: 15–20 mins**

The aromatic star anise gives this very famous traditional Cantonese dish its characteristic flavor, while the dark soy sauce is the secret of the rich and appetizing color.

INGREDIENTS

1 lb 5 oz/600 g pork fillet,
trimmed of all visible fat

2 tbsp dark soy sauce

2 scallions, finely chopped

1-inch/2.5-cm piece fresh gingerroot,
finely chopped

1 tsp red fermented bean curd

2 star anise

1 tbsp Chinese rice wine

1 tbsp honey

1½ tsp Chinese rice vinegar

½ tsp cornstarch

1 tbsp water

NUTRITIONAL INFORMATION

Calories	260
Protein	32g
Carbohydrate	9g
Sugars	5g
Fat	11g
Saturates	4g

cook's tip

Char shiu pork can also be cooked on a barbecue. Cook for 15 minutes over hot coals, turning and brushing frequently with the honey glaze.

1 Brush the pork all over with half the soy sauce and let stand for 15 minutes. Meanwhile, place the scallions, ginger, bean curd, and star anise in a mortar and pound to a paste with a pestle. Transfer to a shallow, nonmetallic dish and stir in the Chinese rice wine, half the honey, 1 teaspoon of the vinegar, and the remaining soy sauce. Add the pork, turning to coat. Cover and let marinate in the refrigerator for 2 hours, turning the pork every 20 minutes.

2 Preheat the oven to 425°F/220°C. Remove the pork from the marinade and pat dry with paper towels. Set aside the marinade. Mix the remaining honey and vinegar with 1 teaspoon of hot water in a bowl and brush the glaze all over the pork. Place the pork on a rack in a roasting pan and roast in the oven for 10–12 minutes, or until the juices run clear when the meat is pierced with the tip of a knife. Turn the pork once during cooking and brush with the remaining honey glaze.

3 Remove the pork from the oven, cover with foil, and let stand for 10 minutes. Meanwhile, bring the reserved marinade to a boil in a pan. Mix the cornstarch and water until smooth, add to the marinade and stir until thickened. Cut the pork across the grain into ¼-inch/5-mm slices. Serve with the marinade for dipping.

griddled pork with orange sauce

cook: 10 mins   **prep: 10 mins, plus 3 hrs marinating**   **serves 4**

In this recipe, the pork is garnished with gremolata, a popular Italian seasoning mixture with a citrus tang, which gives the dish a refreshing summery flavor.

NUTRITIONAL INFORMATION	
Calories	.204
Protein	.26g
Carbohydrate	.2g
Sugars	.1g
Fat	.10g
Saturates	.3g

INGREDIENTS

4 tbsp freshly squeezed orange juice

4 tbsp red wine vinegar

2 garlic cloves, finely chopped

pepper

4 pork steaks, trimmed of all visible fat

olive oil, for brushing

GREMOLATA

3 tbsp finely chopped fresh parsley

grated rind of 1 lime

grated rind of ½ lemon

1 garlic clove, very finely chopped

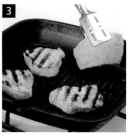

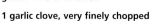

1 Mix the orange juice, vinegar, and garlic together in a shallow, nonmetallic dish and season to taste with pepper. Add the pork, turning to coat. Cover and let marinate in the refrigerator for up to 3 hours.

2 Meanwhile, mix all the gremolata ingredients together in a small mixing bowl, cover with plastic wrap, and let chill in the refrigerator until required.

3 Heat a nonstick griddle pan and brush lightly with olive oil. Remove the pork from the marinade, reserving the marinade, add to the pan and cook over medium–high heat for 5 minutes on each side, or until the juices run clear when the meat is pierced with the tip of a sharp knife.

4 Meanwhile, pour the marinade into a small pan and let simmer over medium heat for 5 minutes, or until slightly thickened. Transfer the pork to a serving dish, pour the orange sauce over it, and sprinkle with the gremolata. Serve immediately.

variation

This dish would work equally well with chicken breast portions. Remove the skin from the cooked chicken before serving.

pork with fennel & anise

serves 4 **prep: 20 mins** ⏲ **cook: 35 mins** ⏲

Lean pork chops, stuffed with an anise and orange filling, are pan-cooked with fennel in an anise-flavored sweet sauce.

INGREDIENTS

4 lean pork chops, about
4½ oz/125 g each
½ cup cooked brown rice
1 tsp orange rind, grated
4 scallions, finely chopped
salt and pepper
½ tsp anise
1 tbsp olive oil

1 fennel bulb, trimmed
and thinly sliced
2 cups unsweetened
orange juice
1 tbsp cornstarch
2 tbsp Pernod
fennel fronds, to garnish
cooked vegetables, to serve

NUTRITIONAL INFORMATION	
Calories	.298
Protein	.30g
Carbohydrate	.18g
Sugars	.10g
Fat	.10g
Saturates	.3g

variation

If you find the anise flavor slightly too intense, then omit the Pernod and blend the cornstarch with 2 tablespoons of water instead.

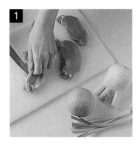

cook's tip

To prepare fennel, rinse under cold running water. Using a sharp knife, cut off the base and the tops, reserving the feathery fronds for garnish. Remove the tough outer leaves and slice lengthwise.

1 Using a sharp knife, trim away any excess fat from the pork chops and make a slit in the center of each chop to create a pocket.

2 Mix the rice, orange rind, scallions, salt and pepper, and anise together in a bowl. Push the rice mixture into the pocket of each chop, then press to seal.

3 Heat the olive oil in a skillet and cook the pork chops on each side for 2–3 minutes, or until lightly browned. Add the fennel and orange juice to the skillet, bring to a boil, and let simmer for 15–20 minutes, or until the meat is tender and cooked through. Remove the pork and fennel with a slotted spoon and transfer to a serving plate.

4 Blend the cornstarch and Pernod together in a small bowl. Add the cornstarch mixture to the skillet and stir into the pan juices. Cook for 2–3 minutes, stirring, until the sauce thickens. Pour the Pernod sauce over the pork chops, garnish with fennel fronds, and serve immediately with freshly cooked vegetables.

pork with plums

serves 4　　　**prep: 15 mins, plus** 🕐 **30 mins marinating**　　　**cook: 25 mins** 🕐

Plum sauce is often used in Chinese cooking with pork, duck or other rich meat to counteract the flavor.

INGREDIENTS

1 lb/450 g pork fillet
1 tbsp cornstarch
2 tbsp light soy sauce
2 tbsp Chinese rice wine
4 tsp light brown sugar
pinch of ground cinnamon
5 tsp vegetable oil
2 garlic cloves, crushed
2 scallions, chopped
4 tbsp plum sauce
1 tbsp hoisin sauce
⅔ cup water
dash of chili sauce
cooked plum quarters (see Cook's Tip)
scallion slices, to garnish

NUTRITIONAL INFORMATION

Calories 281
Protein 25g
Carbohydrate 10g
Sugars 6g
Fat 11g
Saturates 4g

cook's tip

For the garnish, cut 2 ripe plums into quarters. Heat 2 teaspoons of oil in a hot wok or skillet and add the plums. Stir-fry for a few minutes, then remove and drain on paper towels.

1 Cut the pork fillet into thin slices. Mix the cornstarch, soy sauce, Chinese rice wine, sugar, and cinnamon together in a small bowl.

2 Place the pork in a shallow, nonmetallic dish and pour the cornstarch mixture over it. Toss the meat in the marinade until it is completely coated. Cover with plastic wrap and let marinate in the refrigerator for at least 30 minutes.

3 Using a slotted spoon, remove the pork from the dish, reserving the marinade. Heat the vegetable oil in a preheated wok or large skillet. Add the pork and stir-fry for 3–4 minutes, or until a light golden color.

4 Stir in the garlic, scallions, plum sauce, hoisin sauce, water, and chili sauce and bring to a boil. Reduce the heat, cover, and let simmer for 8–10 minutes, or until the pork is cooked through and tender.

5 Stir in the reserved marinade and cook, stirring, for 5 minutes.

6 Transfer the pork stir-fry to a warmed serving dish and garnish with cooked plum quarters and scallion slices. Serve immediately.

pork stroganoff

🕙 cook: 30 mins   🕘 prep: 20 mins   serves 4

Tender, lean pork, cooked in a delicious rich tomato sauce is flavored with the extra tang of plain yogurt.

NUTRITIONAL INFORMATION	
Calories	223
Protein	22g
Carbohydrate	12g
Sugars	7g
Fat	10g
Saturates	3g

INGREDIENTS

12 oz/350 g lean pork fillet

1 tbsp vegetable oil

1 medium onion, chopped

2 garlic cloves, crushed

2 tbsp all-purpose flour

2 tbsp tomato paste

generous 1¾ cups Chicken or Vegetable
Stock (see page 11)

4½ oz/125 g white mushrooms, sliced

1 large green bell pepper, seeded

salt and pepper

½ tsp freshly grated nutmeg, plus extra
to garnish

4 tbsp lowfat plain yogurt

boiled rice with chopped fresh parsley,
to serve

cook's tip

You can buy ready-made stock
from leading supermarkets.
Although more expensive,
this is more nutritious than
bouillon cubes, which are high
in salt and artificial flavorings.

1 Trim away any excess fat and silver skin from the pork, then cut the meat into ½-inch/1-cm thick slices. Heat the vegetable oil in a large, heavy-bottom skillet and gently cook the pork, onion, and garlic for 4–5 minutes, or until lightly browned.

2 Stir in the flour and tomato paste, then

pour in the Chicken Stock and stir to mix thoroughly. Add the mushrooms, bell pepper, salt and pepper to taste, and nutmeg. Bring to a boil, cover, and let simmer for 20 minutes, or until the pork is tender and cooked through.

3 Remove the skillet from the heat and stir in the yogurt. Transfer the pork to

4 large, warmed serving plates and serve with boiled rice sprinkled with chopped fresh parsley and an extra spoonful of yogurt, garnished with freshly grated nutmeg.

lamb tagine

serves 4   **prep: 10 mins**   **cook: 1 hr 40 mins**

This is a typical Moroccan mixture of meat, vegetables, and apricots, flavored with plenty of fresh herbs and spices. It is delicious—and authentic—if served with couscous, which can be cooked in a steamer set over the stew for 6–7 minutes.

INGREDIENTS

1 tbsp corn oil	1 cinnamon stick
1 onion, chopped	½-inch/1-cm piece fresh gingerroot,
12 oz/350 g boneless lamb,	finely chopped
trimmed of all visible fat and	1 eggplant
cut into 1-inch/2.5-cm cubes	4 tomatoes, peeled and chopped
1 garlic clove, finely chopped	⅔ cup no-soak dried apricots
2½ cups Vegetable Stock	2 tbsp chopped fresh cilantro
(see page 11)	salt and pepper
grated rind and juice of 1 orange	freshly cooked couscous, to serve
1 tsp honey	

NUTRITIONAL INFORMATION

Calories	267
Protein	21g
Carbohydrate	22g
Sugars	21g
Fat	11g
Saturates	4g

variation

This stew can also be made with the same quantity of no-soak prunes. Alternatively, add ⅓ cup no-soak apricots and ⅓ cup raisins.

cook's tip

Large eggplants benefit from being sprinkled with salt and left to stand for 30 minutes to remove the bitter juices. Smaller eggplants can be used without salting.

1 Heat the corn oil in a large, heavy-bottom skillet or ovenproof casserole. Add the onion and lamb cubes and cook over medium heat, stirring frequently, for 5 minutes, or until the meat is lightly browned all over. Add the chopped garlic, Vegetable Stock, orange rind and juice, honey, cinnamon stick, and gingerroot. Bring to a boil,

then reduce the heat, cover with a lid and let simmer for 45 minutes.

2 Using a sharp knife, halve the eggplant lengthwise and slice thinly. Add to the skillet with the chopped tomatoes and apricots. Cover and cook for an additional 45 minutes, or until the lamb is tender.

3 Stir in the cilantro, season to taste with salt and pepper and serve immediately, straight from the skillet, with the freshly cooked couscous.

greek lamb pockets

serves 4 **prep: 25 mins,** plus 8 hrs marinating **cook: 35 mins**

Steaming is an excellent lowfat cooking technique. It is essential that the steamer has a tight-fitting lid. If it doesn't, wrap a clean dish towel round the lid to ensure it fits snugly.

INGREDIENTS

1 lb 2 oz/500 g boneless lamb, trimmed of all visible fat and cut into small cubes

2 tsp olive oil

1 red bell pepper, seeded and finely chopped

4 tomatoes, peeled and coarsely chopped

1 eggplant, coarsely chopped

1 zucchini, coarsely chopped

4 shallots, cut into wedges

salt and pepper

1 tbsp chopped fresh mint

1 tbsp snipped fresh chives

generous ⅓ cup Vegetable Stock (see page 11)

½ cup lowfat plain yogurt

fresh rosemary sprigs, to garnish

MARINADE

4 tsp mavrodaphne or sweet sherry

1 shallot, finely chopped

1 garlic clove, finely chopped

1 tsp olive oil

salt and pepper

NUTRITIONAL INFORMATION

Calories	.310
Protein	.30g
Carbohydrate	.12g
Sugars	.11g
Fat	.14g
Saturates	.6g

variation

Boneless leg of lamb is also ideal for this dish. If shallots are unavailable, replace with 1 sliced onion.

cook's tip

During the marinating process, turn the meat occasionally with a slotted spoon. Before cooking, drain the meat thoroughly and bring it to room temperature.

1 Place the lamb in a nonmetallic dish. Mix all the marinade ingredients together in a bowl, seasoning to taste. Pour the marinade over the lamb, turning to coat well. Cover and let marinate in the refrigerator for 8 hours, or preferably overnight. Remove from the marinade and pat dry with paper towels. Set aside the marinade.

2 Heat the olive oil in a heavy-bottom skillet. Add the lamb and cook, stirring, for 5 minutes, or until browned. Stir in the bell pepper, tomatoes, eggplant, zucchini, and shallots, and season to taste. Cut a piece of foil large enough to contain the lamb mixture and spoon the mixture onto it, sprinkle with half the mint and half the chives and turn up the edges of the foil. Return the pan to the heat, add the stock and bring to a boil, scraping up any sediment on the bottom. Boil until thickened, then pour over the lamb. Seal the foil pocket and place in a steamer set over a pan of boiling water. Cover and let steam for 30 minutes, topping up with more water, if necessary.

3 Meanwhile, bring the marinade to a boil in a pan. Stir in the remaining mint and chives, then remove from the heat and let cool. Transfer the lamb mixture to a warmed dish. Stir the yogurt into the marinade and pour over the lamb. Garnish with rosemary sprigs and serve.

swedish lamb stew

serves 4   **prep: 15 mins** ⟲   **cook: 2 hrs** ⟱

This hearty, dill-flavored lamb stew is a welcome sight on a cold winter evening. Serve with steamed vegetables and plenty of crusty bread to mop up the delicious juices, if you like.

INGREDIENTS

1 lb/450 g boneless lamb
salt and white pepper
1 onion, cut into wedges
2 fresh dill sprigs
1 bay leaf
6 green peppercorns
1 fennel bulb, thinly sliced

4 oz/115 g puffball mushrooms
2 tsp cornstarch
1 tbsp skim milk
grated rind and juice of ½ lemon
⅔ cup strained plain yogurt
1 tsp mild mustard
4 tbsp snipped fresh dill

NUTRITIONAL INFORMATION	
Calories	276
Protein	28g
Carbohydrate	11g
Sugars	5g
Fat	14g
Saturates	7g

variation

If you prefer, you can substitute whole white mushrooms for the puffball mushrooms.

cook's tip

If you have more cooking liquid than you require in Step 2, cool and freeze the excess to use in another lamb dish. As lamb stock is strongly flavored, do not use it with other types of meat or poultry.

1 Using a sharp knife, trim off all visible fat from the lamb and cut into 1-inch/2.5-cm cubes. Place the lamb in a large pan and cover with cold water. Add a pinch of salt. Bring to a boil over medium heat and, using a slotted spoon, skim off any scum that rises to the surface. Add the onion, dill sprigs, bay leaf, and peppercorns. Reduce the heat, cover, and let simmer for 45 minutes. Add the fennel and mushrooms, cover, and let simmer for 30 minutes, or until the lamb is very tender.

2 Using a slotted spoon, transfer the lamb, onion, fennel, and mushrooms to a dish and keep warm. Strain the cooking liquid and set aside 1¼ cups. Rinse the pan, pour in the cooking liquid and bring to a boil. Mix the cornstarch and milk until smooth and stir into the sauce. Reduce the heat and let simmer, stirring, for 5 minutes, or until thickened. Stir in the lemon rind and juice.

3 Return the lamb, onion, fennel, and mushrooms to the pan and let simmer, uncovered, for 5 minutes. Meanwhile, mix the yogurt, mustard, and snipped fresh dill together in a small bowl and season to taste with salt and pepper. Stir the yogurt mixture into the stew, transfer to a warmed serving dish, and serve immediately.

chicken with saffron mash

serves 4   **prep: 20 mins** ⟲   **cook: 25 mins** ⟳

The addition of fresh thyme, cilantro, and lemon juice complements the griddled chicken and saffron mash to perfection. Serve with freshly cooked steamed vegetables, such as carrots, broccoli, and green beans, if you like.

INGREDIENTS

1 lb 4 oz/550 g mealy potatoes, cut into chunks

1 garlic clove, peeled

1 tsp saffron threads, crushed

5 cups Chicken or Vegetable Stock (see page 11)

4 skinless, boneless chicken breasts, trimmed of all visible fat

2 tbsp olive oil

1 tbsp lemon juice

1 tbsp chopped fresh thyme

1 tbsp chopped fresh cilantro

1 tbsp coriander seeds, crushed

⅓ cup hot skim milk

salt and pepper

fresh thyme sprigs, to garnish

NUTRITIONAL INFORMATION	
Calories	310
Protein	31g
Carbohydrate	25g
Sugars	2g
Fat	10g
Saturates	2g

variation

Serve sweet potato cream instead. Bake 1 lb 4 oz/550 g sweet potatoes for 1 hour. Scoop out the flesh and mash. Heat and stir in a little butter.

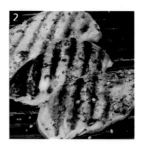

cook's tip

Set aside the stock when you drain the potatoes. Reheat, stirring in 1 tablespoon of chopped fresh thyme and salt and pepper to taste, then serve as a soup.

1 Put the potatoes, garlic, and saffron in a large heavy-bottom pan, add the stock and bring to a boil. Cover and let simmer for 20 minutes, or until tender.

2 Meanwhile, brush the chicken breasts all over with half the olive oil and all of the lemon juice. Sprinkle with the fresh thyme, cilantro, and the crushed coriander seeds. Heat a griddle pan, add the chicken and cook over medium–high heat for 5 minutes on each side, or until the juices run clear when the meat is pierced with the tip of a sharp knife. Alternatively, cook the chicken breasts under a preheated medium–hot broiler for 5 minutes on each side, or until cooked through.

3 Drain the potatoes and return the contents of the strainer to the pan. Add the remaining olive oil and the milk, season to taste with salt and pepper and mash until smooth. Divide the saffron mash between 4 large, warmed serving plates, top with a piece of chicken, and garnish with a few sprigs of fresh thyme. Serve.

minty lime chicken

serves 6   **prep: 35 mins,** ⌚ **plus 30 mins marinating**   **cook: 20 mins** ⏲

These tasty, tangy lime and honey-coated chicken pieces have a matching sauce or dip based on creamy plain yogurt. Served with a fresh, crisp salad they are perfect for a filling lunch or light supper.

INGREDIENTS

3 tbsp finely chopped fresh mint

4 tbsp honey

4 tbsp lime juice

salt and pepper

12 boneless chicken thighs

mixed salad, to serve

SAUCE

⅔ cup lowfat plain thick yogurt

1 tbsp finely chopped fresh mint

2 tsp finely grated lime rind

NUTRITIONAL INFORMATION

Calories	170
Protein	23g
Carbohydrate	12g
Sugars	12g
Fat	3g
Saturates	2g

cook's tip

When cooking chicken pieces under the hot broiler or over the barbecue, do not line the broiler or grill rack with foil as it may catch some fat, then catch fire.

1 Mix the mint, honey, and lime juice in a large bowl and season to taste with salt and pepper. Use toothpicks to keep the chicken thighs in neat shapes and add the chicken to the marinade, turning to coat evenly.

2 Cover with plastic wrap and let the chicken marinate in the refrigerator for at least 30 minutes, longer if possible. Remove the chicken from the marinade and drain. Set aside the marinade.

3 Preheat the broiler to medium. Place the chicken on a broiler rack and cook under the hot broiler for 15–18 minutes, or until the chicken is tender and the juices run clear when a tip of a knife is inserted into the thickest part of the meat. Turn the chicken frequently and baste with the marinade. Alternatively, cook over hot coals on a lit barbecue.

4 Meanwhile, combine all the sauce ingredients in a bowl. Remove the toothpicks and serve with a salad and the sauce for dipping.

spicy tomato chicken

cook: 10 mins   **prep: 10 mins, plus 30 mins soaking**   serves 4

These lowfat, spicy skewers are cooked in a matter of minutes—assemble ahead of time and store in the refrigerator until you need them. They are also ideal cooked on the barbecue.

NUTRITIONAL INFORMATION

Calories 195

Protein 28g

Carbohydrate 12g

Sugars 11g

Fat 4g

Saturates 1g

INGREDIENTS

1 lb 2 oz/500 g skinless, boneless
chicken breasts
3 tbsp tomato paste
2 tbsp honey
2 tbsp Worcestershire sauce
1 tbsp chopped fresh rosemary
9 oz/250 g cherry tomatoes
fresh rosemary sprigs, to garnish
freshly cooked couscous or
rice, to serve

cook's tip

Couscous is made from
semolina that has been made
into separate grains. It usually
just needs moistening or
steaming before serving.

1 Using a sharp knife, cut the chicken into 1-inch/2.5-cm chunks and place in a bowl. Mix the tomato paste, honey, Worcestershire sauce, and rosemary together in a separate bowl, then add to the chicken, stirring to coat evenly.

2 Soak 8 wooden skewers in a bowl of cold water for 30 minutes to prevent them burning during cooking. Preheat the broiler to medium. Thread the chicken pieces and cherry tomatoes alternately onto the skewers and place on a broiler rack.

3 Spoon over any remaining glaze and cook under the preheated hot broiler for 8–10 minutes, turning occasionally, until the chicken is cooked through. Transfer to 4 large serving plates, garnish with a few sprigs of fresh rosemary, and serve with freshly cooked couscous or rice.

pan-fried chicken & cilantro

serves 4   **prep: 15 mins**   **cook: 15 mins**

It is difficult to believe that the rich-tasting sauce coating this flavorsome chicken doesn't contain lots of heavy cream. Nevertheless, this is a lowfat dish and all it needs as an accompaniment is a steamed green vegetable or a crisp salad.

INGREDIENTS

1 bunch of fresh cilantro

1 tbsp corn oil

4 skinless, boneless chicken breasts, about 4 oz/115 g each, trimmed of all visible fat

1 tsp cornstarch

1 tbsp water

⅓ cup lowfat plain yogurt

2 tbsp reduced fat light cream

¾ cup Chicken Stock (see page 11)

2 tbsp lime juice

2 garlic cloves, finely chopped

1 shallot, finely chopped

1 tomato, peeled, seeded, and chopped

salt and pepper

NUTRITIONAL INFORMATION

Calories	200
Protein	27g
Carbohydrate	6g
Sugars	3g
Fat	8g
Saturates	3g

variation

Instead of fresh cilantro, try using fresh tarragon. As tarragon is strongly flavored, only use a few stalks, otherwise it may overpower the dish.

cook's tip

Wrap the chicken portions in pieces of foil to keep warm and to prevent them from drying out after cooking. Before serving, remove from the foil and transfer to plates.

1 Set aside a few cilantro sprigs for a garnish and coarsely chop the remainder. Heat the corn oil in a heavy-bottom skillet, add the chicken and cook over medium heat for 5 minutes on each side, or until the juices run clear when the meat is pierced with the tip of a sharp knife. Remove from the skillet and keep warm.

2 Mix the cornstarch and water until smooth. Stir in the yogurt and cream. Pour the Chicken Stock and lime juice into the skillet and add the garlic and shallot. Reduce the heat and let simmer for 1 minute. Stir the tomato into the yogurt mixture and stir the mixture into the skillet. Season to taste with salt and pepper. Cook, stirring constantly, for 1–2 minutes, or until slightly thickened, but do not let the mixture boil. Stir in the chopped fresh cilantro.

3 Place the chicken on a large serving plate, pour the sauce over it and garnish with the reserved cilantro sprigs. Serve.

chicken with mustard

serves 4   **prep: 10 mins** ⏱   **cook: 20 mins** ⏱

The combination of chicken and a mustard and orange sauce is quite irresistible. Cooking the dish is simplicity itself—and, as an extra benefit, so is clearing up afterward.

INGREDIENTS

1 tbsp corn oil

4 skinless, boneless chicken breasts, about 5 oz/140 g each, all visible fat removed

salt and pepper

2 large oranges, peeled and cut into segments, juice set aside (see Cook's Tip)

2 tsp cornstarch

⅔ cup lowfat plain yogurt

1 tsp whole-grain mustard

fresh parsley leaves, to garnish

NUTRITIONAL INFORMATION

Calories 267

Protein 34g

Carbohydrate 16g

Sugars 12g

Fat 8g

Saturates 2g

---

variation

Omit the oranges and make the sauce with 2 tablespoons of lemon juice and 1 teaspoon of Dijon mustard instead of the whole-grain.

cook's tip

Use a sharp knife to peel the oranges and make sure that you remove all the pith. Hold the oranges over a bowl to catch the juices and cut down between the membranes to separate into segments.

1 Heat the oil in a large, heavy-bottom skillet. Add the chicken breasts and cook over medium–high heat for 5 minutes on each side, or until tender and the juices run clear when the meat is pierced with the tip of a sharp knife. Season with a little salt and pepper, remove the chicken from the skillet, cover with foil, and keep warm.

2 Pour the orange juice into a small bowl and stir in the cornstarch to make a smooth paste. Stir in the yogurt and mustard, then pour into the skillet, and bring to a boil over low heat, stirring constantly.

3 Add the orange segments to the skillet and season to taste with salt and pepper. Stir in any juices that have collected from the chicken. Spoon the sauce onto 4 large, warmed serving plates and top with the chicken. Garnish with parsley leaves and serve immediately.

chicken fricassée

serves 4   **prep: 15 mins**   **cook: 35–40 mins**

While it is typically cooked in cream, the term fricassée merely denotes cooking the meat—or sometimes fish—in a white sauce, without browning it. Serve with plain boiled rice or new potatoes for a filling supper.

INGREDIENTS

1 tbsp all-purpose flour	1 cup Chicken Stock
salt and white pepper	(see page 11)
4 skinless, boneless chicken	2 carrots, diced
breasts, about 5 oz/140 g each,	2 celery stalks, diced
trimmed of all visible fat and	2 cups frozen peas
cut into ¾-inch/2-cm cubes	1 yellow bell pepper, seeded and diced
1 tbsp corn oil	4 oz/115 g white mushrooms, sliced
8 pearl onions	½ cup lowfat plain yogurt
2 garlic cloves, crushed	3 tbsp chopped fresh parsley

NUTRITIONAL INFORMATION

Calories	.287
Protein	.37g
Carbohydrate	.17g
Sugars	.8g
Fat	.8g
Saturates	.2g

variation

You can substitute skim milk for the yogurt and add extra flavor with 1 teaspoon of lemon juice and a pinch of freshly grated nutmeg in Step 3.

cook's tip

When slicing or dicing bell pepper halves, place them on a cutting board, shiny side downward, to prevent the knife from slipping.

1 Spread out the flour on a plate and season with salt and pepper. Add the chicken and, using your hands, coat in the flour. Heat the oil in a heavy-bottom skillet. Add the onions and garlic and cook over low heat, stirring occasionally, for 5 minutes. Add the chicken and cook, stirring, for 10 minutes, or until just starting to color.

2 Gradually stir in the Chicken Stock, then add the carrots, celery, and peas. Bring to a boil, then reduce the heat, cover, and let simmer for 5 minutes. Add the bell pepper and mushrooms, cover, and let simmer for 10 minutes.

3 Stir in the yogurt and chopped parsley and season to taste with salt and pepper. Cook for 1–2 minutes, or until heated through, then transfer to 4 large, warmed serving plates, and serve.

roast turkey with cider sauce

serves 8   **prep: 15 mins,**
plus 10 mins cooling   **cook: 1 hr 40 mins**

Most supermarkets sell boneless turkey breast roast. There is no waste, so it is an economical choice when entertaining and it fits into the oven more easily than a whole bird. Rolling the turkey round the dressing helps to keep it moist during cooking.

INGREDIENTS

1 lb 4 oz/1 kg boneless turkey
breast roast

salt and pepper

1 tbsp corn oil

DRESSING

2 tbsp butter

2 shallots, finely chopped

1 celery stalk, finely chopped

1 cooking apple, peeled,
cored, and diced

⅔ cup prunes, pitted and chopped

⅓ cup raisins

3 tbsp Chicken Stock (see page 11)

4 tbsp hard cider

1 tbsp chopped fresh parsley

SAUCE

1 shallot, very finely chopped

1¼ cups hard cider

½ cup Chicken Stock (see page 11)

1 tsp cider vinegar

variation

Use 3 lb/1.3 kg whole chicken instead.
Fill the neck with dressing and roast for
1½ hours. Roll the remaining dressing
into balls and bake for 15 minutes.

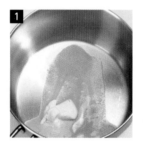

cook's tip

If you want to prepare part
of this dish in advance, make
the dressing the day before
and keep in the refrigerator
until required.

1 Preheat the oven to 375°F/190°C. To make the dressing, melt the butter in a pan. Add the shallots and cook for 5 minutes. Add the celery and apple and cook for 5 minutes. Add the remaining dressing ingredients, cover, and let simmer for 5 minutes, or until all the liquid has been absorbed. Transfer to a bowl and cool.

2 Place the roast on a cutting board and slice almost completely through, from the thin side towards the thicker side. Open out, place between 2 sheets of plastic wrap and flatten with a meat mallet or rolling pin to an even thickness. Season with salt. Spoon on the cooled dressing, roll the roast round it, and tie with string. Heat the oil in a roasting pan over medium heat, add the roast, and brown. Transfer to the oven and roast for 1 hour 10 minutes, or until cooked through and the juices run clear when the meat is pierced with the tip of a knife.

3 Remove the roast from the pan and cover with foil. To make the sauce, pour off any fat from the pan and set over medium heat. Add the shallot and half the cider and cook for 1–2 minutes, scraping any sediment from the bottom of the pan. Add the remaining cider, stock, and vinegar and cook for 10 minutes, or until reduced and thickened. Remove and discard the string from the turkey and cut into slices. Serve with the sauce.

vegetable & tofu stir-fry

serves 4 **prep: 10 mins,** ↺ **plus 2 hrs marinating** **cook: 12 mins** ⏲

Tofu, also known as bean curd, is a lowfat source of high-quality protein for vegetarians. Although it is naturally bland, it absorbs the flavors of other ingredients, especially if it is marinated. Store tofu in the refrigerator, covered with cold water, for up to 3 days, changing the water daily. Drain and pat dry before use.

INGREDIENTS

8 oz/225 g firm tofu (drained weight), cut into bite-size pieces

1 tbsp peanut or corn oil

2 scallions, chopped

1 garlic clove, finely chopped

4 oz/115 g baby corn cobs, halved

1 cup snow peas

4 oz/115 g shiitake mushrooms, thinly sliced

2 tbsp finely chopped fresh cilantro leaves

MARINADE

2 tbsp dark soy sauce

1 tbsp Chinese rice wine

2 tsp brown sugar

½ tsp Chinese five-spice powder

1 fresh red chile, seeded and finely chopped

2 scallions, finely chopped

1 tbsp grated fresh gingerroot

NUTRITIONAL INFORMATION	
Calories	135
Protein	. . . . .11g
Carbohydrate	. . . . .7g
Sugars	. . . . .5g
Fat	. . . . .7g
Saturates	. . . . .3g

variation

Substitute baby carrots, celery, and zucchini, cut into thin sticks, for the baby corn cobs and snow peas.

cook's tip

Always drain firm tofu, because it is packaged in water. Use a small, sharp knife for cutting the tofu—a blunt knife will squash it.

1 Place all the marinade ingredients in a large, shallow, nonmetallic dish and stir to mix. Add the bite-size chunks of tofu and turn them over carefully to coat thoroughly in the marinade. Cover the dish with plastic wrap and leave the tofu in the refrigerator to marinate for 2 hours, turning the chunks over once or twice.

2 Drain the tofu and set aside the marinade. Heat the peanut oil in a preheated wok or large skillet. Add the tofu and stir-fry over medium–high heat for 2–3 minutes, or until golden. Using a slotted spoon, remove the tofu from the wok and set aside. Add the scallions and garlic and stir-fry for 2 minutes, then add the corn cobs and stir-fry for 1 minute. Add the snow peas and mushrooms and stir-fry for an additional 2 minutes.

3 Return the tofu to the wok and add the marinade. Cook gently for 1–2 minutes, or until heated through. Sprinkle with the chopped fresh cilantro and serve immediately.

moroccan vegetable stew

serves 4　　　　**prep: 25 mins** ⏲　　　　**cook: 45 mins** ⏲

This colorful selection of vegetables is simmered in a stock flavored with lots of warming and aromatic spices.

INGREDIENTS

15 oz/425 g canned chickpeas

4 tomatoes, peeled and seeded

3 cups Vegetable Stock
(see page 11)

1 onion, peeled and sliced

2 carrots, peeled and sliced diagonally

1 tbsp chopped fresh cilantro

salt

6 oz/175 g zucchini, sliced

1 small turnip, peeled and cubed

½ tsp ground turmeric

¼ tsp ground ginger

¼ tsp ground cinnamon

1½ cups couscous

fresh cilantro sprigs, to garnish

NUTRITIONAL INFORMATION

Calories	.299
Protein	.13g
Carbohydrate	.56g
Sugars	.7g
Fat	.4g
Saturates	.0g

cook's tip

You can also cook the couscous by putting it into a large heatproof bowl and pouring over enough boiling water to cover. Let stand for 5–8 minutes, then fluff up with a fork and serve.

1 Drain the chickpeas, rinse under cold running water and set aside. Coarsely chop the tomatoes and set aside half. Place the remainder in a blender or food processor and process until a smooth purée forms. Transfer to a large pan and add 1¾ cups of the Vegetable Stock. Bring to a boil, then reduce the heat, and add the onion, carrots, chopped fresh cilantro, and salt to taste. Let simmer, stirring occasionally, for 10 minutes.

2 Stir in the zucchini, turnip, turmeric, ginger, and cinnamon. Partially cover and simmer for an additional 30 minutes. Stir in the reserved chickpeas and let simmer for a few more minutes.

3 Meanwhile, bring the remaining Vegetable Stock to the boil in a heavy-bottom pan. Add a pinch of salt, then sprinkle in the couscous, stirring constantly. Remove the pan from the heat, cover with a tight-fitting lid and let stand for 5 minutes. Fluff up the couscous with a fork and transfer to 4 large serving plates.

Top with the vegetables and their stock, garnish with a few sprigs of fresh cilantro, and serve immediately.

stuffed cabbage rolls

⏲ cook: 1 hr 10 mins   ⏱ prep: 30 mins   serves 4

Bathed in a sweet tomato sauce, these cabbage rolls are stuffed with a nutty filling of pearl barley and zucchinis.

NUTRITIONAL INFORMATION

Calories 224

Protein 6g

Carbohydrate 43g

Sugars 19g

Fat 5g

Saturates 1g

INGREDIENTS

8 large or 12 medium green
cabbage leaves

4 cups water

scant ½ cup pearl barley

2 tbsp chopped fresh parsley

2 garlic cloves, coarsely chopped

1 lb 12 oz/800 g canned chopped tomatoes

4 tbsp red wine vinegar

1 tbsp corn oil, plus
extra for brushing

2 zucchinis, diced

3 scallions, sliced

salt and pepper

2 tbsp brown sugar

cook's tip

Substitute the pearl barley with long-grain rice. Cook the rice with half the parsley in a large pan of boiling water for 18–20 minutes in Step 1. Drain and proceed as in main recipe.

1 Preheat the oven to 375°F/190°C. Cut out the stems from the cabbage leaves, then blanch the leaves in boiling water for 1 minute. Drain and spread out to dry. Bring the water to a boil in a pan. Add the barley and half the parsley. Reduce the heat, cover, and let simmer for 45 minutes, or until the liquid has been absorbed.

2 Meanwhile, put the garlic, 14 oz/400 g of the tomatoes and the vinegar in a blender or food processor and process until smooth. Transfer to a bowl and set aside. Heat the oil in a large skillet. Add the zucchini and the remaining parsley and cook over medium heat for 3 minutes. Add the scallions and cook briefly, then add the

tomato mixture and cook for 10 minutes, or until thickened. Transfer to a bowl.

3 Add the cooked barley to the bowl, season to taste with salt and pepper and stir well. Lightly brush an ovenproof dish with oil. Place a spoonful of the barley mixture at the stem end of a cabbage leaf. Roll up, tucking in the

sides, and place, seam-side down, in the dish. Stuff and roll the remaining cabbage leaves in the same way, placing them in the dish in a single layer. Sprinkle the brown sugar over the rolls and pour the remaining tomatoes, with their can juice, on top. Cover with foil and bake in the oven for 30 minutes, or until tender. Serve straight from the dish.

lemony spaghetti

cook: 25 mins   **prep: 10 mins**   **serves 4**

NUTRITIONAL INFORMATION

Calories 133

Protein 8g

Carbohydrate 25g

Sugars 8g

Fat 1g

Saturates 2g

variation

Replace the lowfat cream cheese with lowfat plain yogurt and add your favorite combination of vegetables, if you prefer.

Steaming vegetables helps to preserve their nutritional content, and allows them to retain their bright, natural colors and crunchy texture. This dish is best served immediately.

INGREDIENTS

8 oz/225 g celery root

2 medium carrots

2 medium leeks

1 small red bell pepper

1 small yellow bell pepper

2 garlic cloves

1 tsp celery seeds

1 tbsp lemon juice

10½ oz/300 g dried spaghetti

celery leaves, chopped, to garnish

DRESSING

1 tsp finely grated lemon rind

1 tbsp lemon juice

4 tbsp lowfat cream cheese

salt and pepper

2 tbsp snipped fresh chives

cook's tip

Use a pair of kitchen scissors to snip chives. Cut the chives over a small bowl and add them at the very end to retain their delicate flavor.

1 To prepare the vegetables, peel the celery root and carrots, then, using a sharp knife, cut into short thin sticks and place in a large bowl. Trim and slice the leeks, rinse under cold running water to flush out any trapped dirt, then shred finely. Halve, seed, and slice the bell peppers and thinly slice the garlic. Add all the vegetables to the bowl

with the celery root and carrots. Add the celery seeds and lemon juice and toss until thoroughly mixed.

2 Cook the spaghetti in a large, heavy-bottom pan of boiling water according to the package instructions, or until tender but still firm to the bite. Drain thoroughly and keep warm.

3 Meanwhile, bring another large pan of water to a boil, place the vegetables in a steamer or meat strainer and place over the boiling water. Cover and steam for 6–7 minutes, or until tender. While the spaghetti and vegetables are cooking, mix all the ingredients for the dressing together. Transfer the spaghetti and vegetables to a

warmed serving bowl or 4 warmed serving plates and mix with the dressing. Garnish with chopped celery leaves and serve immediately.

fish & shellfish

The perfect choice for healthy eating, all fish and shellfish—even so-called oily fish—are naturally low in fat. Nutritionists recommend that we should eat fish two or three times a week, and the recipes featured in this chapter will make that both easy and pleasurable to do. Fish and shellfish are among the most versatile of ingredients and go well with a wide range of vegetables, herbs, and spices, and with cheese, pasta, and rice. The huge choice of fish available today ensures that there is a dish to suit all tastes and budgets.

Recipes range from familiar favorites, such as Smoked Haddock Pie (see page 176) and Mussels in White Wine (see page 198) to more unusual dishes, such as Cajun-Spiced Fish (see page 194) and Sea Trout in a Salt Crust (see page 195). There are fabulous fish stews, such as Louisiana Gumbo (see page 184), hot and spicy dishes, such as Indian Chili Fish (see page 181), easy midweek suppers, such as Cod with Cheese & Tomatoes (see page 166), and flamboyant combinations for entertaining, such as Bouillabaisse (see page 196).

In many of the recipes, there is no reason why you shouldn't substitute your own favorite fish for the one suggested. If sole seems too extravagant, use flounder or brill. If you can't find swordfish steaks, try the same recipe with the humble cod. If you are lucky enough to find affordable fresh langoustines, use them in one of the shrimp recipes. The happy fact is that, whatever fish you choose, you will be cooking a delicious and lowfat dish.

cod provençal

serves 4   **prep: 10 mins**   **cook: 15 mins**

Easy to prepare and easy to eat—that is the keynote to this tasty fish dish. As it is also packed with protein and vitamins and contains hardly any saturated fat, you could not make a better choice for a quick and healthy midweek supper.

INGREDIENTS

4 cod steaks, about 5 oz/140 g each

⅔ cup Fish Stock (see page 11)

1 bay leaf

6 black peppercorns

strip of thinly pared lemon rind

2 thin slices of onion

SAUCE

14 oz/400 g canned chopped tomatoes

1 garlic clove, very finely chopped

1 tbsp sun-dried tomato paste

1 tbsp capers, drained and rinsed

16 black olives, pitted

salt and pepper

TO GARNISH

fresh flatleaf parsley sprigs

lemon wedges

NUTRITIONAL INFORMATION	
Calories	168
Protein	. . . . .23g
Carbohydrate	. . . . .4g
Sugars	. . . . .3g
Fat	. . . . .7g
Saturates	. . . . .1g

variation

Add a dash of Pernod to the tomato sauce in Step 3 to give the dish a little extra flavor.

cook's tip

If you don't have any freshly made Fish Stock, you can use a mixture of equal parts dry white wine and water, which works just as well.

1 First, make the sauce. Put the chopped tomatoes, garlic, tomato paste, capers, olives, and salt and pepper to taste in a large, heavy-bottom pan over low heat. Heat gently, stirring occasionally.

2 Meanwhile, place the fish in a shallow, ovenproof casserole in a single layer. Pour in the Fish Stock and add the bay leaf, peppercorns, lemon rind, and onion slices. Bring to a boil, then reduce the heat to very low, cover, and let simmer gently for 10 minutes, or until the fish is opaque and flakes easily when tested with the tip of a knife. Using a fish slice, transfer the cod to a serving plate and keep warm.

3 Strain the stock into the sauce and stir over medium heat until slightly reduced. Pour the sauce over the fish, then garnish with a few sprigs of fresh parsley and lemon wedges. Serve.

fragrant tuna steaks

cook: 10–15 mins   **prep: 15 mins**   **serves 4**

<table>
<tr><td colspan="2">NUTRITIONAL INFORMATION</td></tr>
<tr><td>Calories</td><td>.239</td></tr>
<tr><td>Protein</td><td>.42g</td></tr>
<tr><td>Carbohydrate</td><td>.0.5g</td></tr>
<tr><td>Sugars</td><td>.0.1g</td></tr>
<tr><td>Fat</td><td>.8g</td></tr>
<tr><td>Saturates</td><td>.2g</td></tr>
</table>

variation

Fresh salmon steaks would work equally well for this dish and substitute the lime rind and juice for lemon.

Fresh tuna steaks are very meaty—they have a firm texture, yet the flesh is succulent. Steaks from the belly are best of all. Tuna is very rich in valuable Omega-3 oils.

INGREDIENTS

4 tuna steaks, about 6 oz/175 g each

½ tsp finely grated lime rind

1 garlic clove, crushed

2 tsp olive oil

1 tsp ground cumin

1 tsp ground coriander

pepper

1 tbsp lime juice

1 tbsp chopped fresh cilantro, to garnish

TO SERVE

avocado relish (see Cook's Tip)

tomato wedges

lime wedges

cook's tip

For the relish, peel and chop a small avocado. Mix in 1 tablespoon lime juice, 1 tablespoon chopped cilantro, 1 chopped red onion, and some chopped tomato. Season to taste.

1 Using a sharp knife, trim the skin from the tuna steaks, rinse under cold running water, and pat dry with paper towels.

2 Mix the lime rind, garlic, olive oil, ground cumin, ground coriander, and pepper together in a bowl to make a paste and spread thinly on both sides of the tuna.

3 Heat a nonstick ridged griddle pan until hot and press the tuna steaks into the pan to seal them. Reduce the heat and cook for 5 minutes. Turn the fish steaks over and cook for an additional 4–5 minutes, or until the fish is cooked through. Remove the fish from the griddle pan and drain on paper towels. Transfer to a serving plate.

4 Sprinkle the lime juice and chopped fresh cilantro over the fish. Serve with the avocado relish and tomato and lime wedges.

italian sardines

serves 4 **prep: 20 mins** **cook: 8–10 mins**

Although they can be awkward and time-consuming to deal with, fresh sardines are a real treat. They are best cooked very simply— even just cleaned and broiled or barbecued. Here they are flavored with garlic and lemon rind and served with bruschetta. They go well with a tomato and onion salad.

INGREDIENTS

1 tbsp olive oil

4 garlic cloves

1 lb 7 oz/650 g fresh sardines, cleaned and scaled (see Cook's Tip)

grated rind of 2 lemons

2 tbsp chopped fresh flatleaf parsley

salt and pepper

tomato and onion salad, to serve

BRUSCHETTA

4 thick slices of ciabatta or other rustic bread

2 garlic cloves, halved

2 large tomatoes, halved

NUTRITIONAL INFORMATION

Calories 405

Protein 38g

Carbohydrate 23g

Sugars 4g

Fat 19g

Saturates 5g

---

variation

A variety of toppings can be used for the bruschetta. Try broiled bell pepper with fresh basil. Replace the ciabatta with French bread slices.

cook's tip

To clean sardines, slit open the belly and remove the insides. Rinse and dry. To scale, hold the fish by its tail under running water and run your hand along the body from tail to head.

1 Preheat the broiler to medium. Heat the olive oil in a large, heavy-bottom skillet. Add the garlic and cook over low heat until softened. Meanwhile, for the bruschetta, put the bread under the preheated hot broiler and toast lightly on both sides. Transfer to a heatproof plate and keep warm in a low oven until required.

2 Add the sardines to the skillet and cook for 5 minutes, turning once. Sprinkle with the grated lemon rind and chopped fresh parsley, and season to taste with salt and pepper.

3 To finish the bruschetta, rub 1 side of each slice of toast with the cut side of a garlic clove, then with the cut side of a tomato. Divide the bruschetta and sardines between 4 serving plates and serve immediately with a tomato and onion salad.

cod with cheese & tomatoes

serves 4 **prep: 10 mins, plus** ⏲ **30 mins marinating** **cook: 25 mins** ⏲

Fish and cheese have a natural affinity, but recipes usually suggest adding creamy sauces with the result that the fat content starts to soar. Here, fish is oven-baked, topped with cheese and broiled.

INGREDIENTS

4 cod or other firm white fish fillets, about 6 oz/175 g each

grated rind and juice of 1 orange

8 canned anchovy fillets, drained and patted dry

6 oz/175 g haloumi or provolone cheese

4 beefsteak tomato slices

fresh parsley sprigs, to garnish

NUTRITIONAL INFORMATION

Calories	159
Protein	19g
Carbohydrate	6g
Sugars	6g
Fat	7g
Saturates	4g

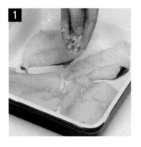

cook's tip

Citrus juices will start to "cure" fish after 1 hour, so make sure that you don't leave the fish to marinate for too long.

1 Place the fish in a large, shallow, nonmetallic ovenproof dish. Sprinkle with the orange rind and pour the juice over it. Cover with plastic wrap and let marinate in the refrigerator for 30 minutes.

2 Preheat the oven to 350°F/180°C. Remove the plastic wrap and

re-cover the dish with foil. Bake in the preheated oven for 15–20 minutes, or until the flesh flakes easily.

3 Preheat the broiler to medium. Drain the anchovy fillets on paper towels and arrange 2 fillets on each piece of cod. Place under a preheated broiler for 1 minute. Cut the cheese into 4 slices

and place 1 slice on top of each cod fillet. Top with the tomato slices and return to the broiler for an additional 1–2 minutes, or until the cheese has charred slightly and the tomato is starting to soften. Transfer to a serving plate, garnish with a few sprigs of fresh parsley, and serve immediately.

angler fish with coconut

🕒 **cook: 20–25 mins**　　　🕒 **prep: 30 mins, plus 4 hrs marinating**　　　**serves 4**

These are tasty kabobs with a mild marinade. Allow the skewers to marinate for at least 1 hour before cooking. Serve with a crisp salad or freshly cooked rice as part of a buffet or summer barbecue.

NUTRITIONAL INFORMATION	
Calories	193
Protein	39g
Carbohydrate	2g
Sugars	2g
Fat	3g
Saturates	1g

INGREDIENTS

1 lb/450 g angler fish tails

8 oz/225 g raw shelled shrimp

dry unsweetened coconut, toasted, to garnish (optional)

MARINADE

1 tsp corn oil

½ small onion, finely grated

1 tsp fresh gingerroot, grated

⅔ cup canned coconut milk

2 tbsp chopped fresh cilantro

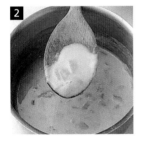

cook's tip

If using wooden skewers, remember to soak then in a bowl of cold water for 30 minutes to prevent them burning during cooking.

1 To make the marinade, heat the corn oil in a large, heavy-bottom pan and cook the onion and ginger for 5 minutes, until just softened but not browned.

2 Add the coconut milk to the pan and bring to a boil. Boil rapidly for 5 minutes, or until reduced to the consistency of light cream.

Remove from the heat and let cool completely.

3 When cooled, stir the cilantro into the coconut milk and pour into a shallow dish. Cut the fish into bite-size chunks and stir into the coconut mixture together with the shrimp. Cover and let marinate in the refrigerator for 1–4 hours.

4 Preheat the broiler to medium. Thread the fish and shrimp onto metal or presoaked wooden skewers and discard any remaining marinade. Cook the skewers under the preheated hot broiler for 10–15 minutes, turning frequently. Alternatively, cook over hot coals on a lit barbecue. Garnish with toasted coconut and serve.

sweet-&-sour fish

serves 4   **prep: 10 mins** ⟲   **cook: 35 mins** ⟳

East meets West with this delicious fish bake. The combination of the dark soy sauce, pineapple, and bell peppers gives the fish a wonderful flavor, and is a real treat on any occasion.

INGREDIENTS

1 red bell pepper	8 oz/225 g canned pineapple
1 green bell pepper	cubes in syrup
3 tbsp dark soy sauce	2 tomatoes, peeled and chopped
4 tbsp white wine vinegar	6 oz/175 g white mushrooms,
1 tbsp tomato paste	thinly sliced
1 cup Fish Stock	salt and pepper
(see page 11) or water	1 lb 7 oz/650 g white
2 tsp cornstarch	fish fillets, skinned

NUTRITIONAL INFORMATION

Calories 192
Protein 30g
Carbohydrate 16g
Sugars 14g
Fat 2g
Saturates 0g

variation

You can use any firm-fleshed white fish fillets in this dish. Try haddock, cod, angler fish, or whiting.

cook's tip

To skin a fish fillet, secure it on a board with salt. Insert a sharp, flexible knife at one end and hold firmly. Move the knife along the length of the fillet in a cutting motion against the skin.

1 Preheat the oven to 350°/180°C. Prepare the bell peppers. Using a sharp knife, halve each bell pepper, remove the core, seed, and cut into thin sticks. Put the soy sauce, vinegar, and tomato paste in a pan. Put 4 tablespoons of the Fish Stock in a small bowl and add the remainder to the pan. Stir the cornstarch into the reserved

fish stock to make a smooth paste. Bring the mixture in the pan to a boil, stir in the cornstarch paste and cook over low heat, stirring constantly, until thickened. Let simmer for 5 minutes.

2 Add the reserved bell peppers, pineapple cubes and syrup, tomatoes, and mushrooms to the pan

and cook, stirring occasionally, for 5 minutes. Season to taste with salt and pepper

3 Arrange the fish fillets in the bottom of a shallow ovenproof dish. Spoon the sauce mixture on top and cover with foil. Bake in the oven for 20 minutes, or until the fish flakes easily. Serve.

yucatan fish

serves 4 **prep: 10 mins,** plus 30 mins marinating **cook: 40 mins**

Plenty of fresh herbs, onion, green bell pepper, and pepitas are used to flavor this delicious baked fish dish, which is first marinated in a little lime juice. Serve straight from the oven with freshly cooked rice or steamed broccoli, if you like.

INGREDIENTS

4 cod or hake steaks, about 6 oz/175 g each

2 tbsp lime juice

salt and pepper

1 green bell pepper

1 tbsp olive oil

1 onion, chopped finely

1–2 garlic cloves, crushed

2 tbsp green pepitas

grated rind of ½ lime

1 tbsp chopped fresh cilantro or parsley

1 tbsp chopped fresh mixed herbs

2 oz/55 g white mushrooms, thinly sliced

2–3 tbsp fresh orange juice or white wine

TO GARNISH

lime wedges

fresh mixed herbs

NUTRITIONAL INFORMATION

Calories	.248
Protein	.33g
Carbohydrate	.3g
Sugars	.2g
Fat	.11g
Saturates	.1g

variation

Replace the cod steaks with a whole cleaned fish, such as red snapper or rainbow trout.

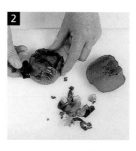

cook's tip

When marinating fish in lime juice, do not leave for longer than the recipe states, otherwise the lime juice will start to preserve it.

1 Wipe the fish with paper towels, place in a shallow ovenproof dish and pour over the lime juice. Turn the fish in the juice, season with salt and pepper, cover, and let marinate in the refrigerator for 15–30 minutes.

2 Preheat the broiler to medium. Halve the bell pepper, remove the seeds, and place under the preheated hot broiler, skin-side upward, until the skin burns and splits. Let cool slightly, then peel off the skin and chop the flesh.

3 Preheat the oven to 350°F/180°C. Heat the olive oil in a skillet and cook the onion, garlic, bell pepper, and pepitas until the onion is soft.

4 Stir in the lime rind, chopped cilantro or parsley, mixed herbs, mushrooms, and salt and pepper to taste, then spoon over the fish. Spoon or pour the orange juice or wine over the fish, cover, and cook in the preheated oven for 30 minutes, or until the fish is just tender. Garnish with lime wedges and herbs and serve.

piquant fish cakes

⏲ **cook: 50 mins**   🕐 **prep: 30 mins, plus 1 hr chilling**   **serves 4**

NUTRITIONAL INFORMATION

Calories	334
Protein	. . . . .31g
Carbohydrate	. . . . .37g
Sugars	. . . . .7g
Fat	. . . . .7g
Saturates	. . . . .1g

variation

For a change, replace the piquant sauce with either homemade or store-bought tartar sauce.

The combination of pink- and white-fleshed fish, with a tasty tomato sauce, transforms the humble fish into something extra special. Serve with fresh salad greens and lemon wedges.

INGREDIENTS

1 lb/450 g potatoes, diced

8 oz/225 g trout fillet

8 oz/225 g haddock fillet

1 bay leaf

generous 1¼ cups Fish Stock (see page 11)

2 tbsp lowfat cream cheese

4 tbsp snipped fresh chives

salt and pepper

scant ¾ cup dry white bread crumbs

1 tbsp corn oil

fresh chives, to garnish

SAUCE

generous ¾ cup strained tomatoes

4 tbsp dry white wine

4 tbsp lowfat plain yogurt

chili powder

TO SERVE

lemon wedges

salad greens

cook's tip

The best utensil for mashing potatoes is a potato masher. However, if you do not have one, a fork works just as well. Make sure the potatoes are well drained.

1 Cook the potatoes in a pan of boiling water for 10 minutes, or until tender. Drain and mash.

2 Meanwhile, place the fish in another large pan with the bay leaf and Fish Stock. Bring to a boil and let simmer for 7–8 minutes, or until tender.

3 Remove the fish with a slotted spoon and flake the flesh away from the skin. Mix the fish with the potato, cream cheese, chives, and salt and pepper to taste. Cool, then cover and let chill for 1 hour.

4 Sprinkle the bread crumbs on a plate. Divide the fish mixture into 8 and form each portion into a patty, 3 inches/7.5 cm in diameter. Press each fish cake into the bread crumbs, coating all over. Brush a skillet with corn oil and cook the fish cakes for 6 minutes. Turn the fish cakes over and cook for an additional 5–6 minutes, or until golden. Drain on paper towels and keep warm.

5 To make the sauce, heat the strained tomatoes and wine in a small pan. Season, then remove from the heat and stir in the yogurt. Return to the heat, then transfer to a bowl and sprinkle with chili powder. Garnish the fish cakes with chives and serve with lemon wedges, salad greens, and the sauce.

five-spice salmon

serves 4 **prep: 15 mins** ⟲ **cook: 10–15 mins** ⟲

Five-spice powder is a blend of star anise, fennel, cinnamon, cloves, and Szechuan pepper that is often used in Chinese dishes.

INGREDIENTS

4 salmon fillets, skinned, about
4½ oz/125 g each

2 tsp Chinese five-spice powder

salt and pepper

1 large leek

1 large carrot

4 oz/115 g snow peas

1-inch/2.5-cm piece fresh gingerroot

2 tbsp ginger wine

2 tbsp light soy sauce

1 tbsp vegetable oil

NUTRITIONAL INFORMATION

Calories 267

Protein 24g

Carbohydrate 4g

Sugars 3g

Fat 17g

Saturates 3g

cook's tip

Chinese five-spice powder is strong and pungent and should be used sparingly as it may overpower the finished dish.

1 Rinse the salmon under cold running water and pat dry on paper towels. Rub the Chinese five-spice powder into both sides of the fish and season to taste with salt and pepper. Set aside.

2 Trim the leek, slice it down the center and rinse under cold running water to remove dirt. Finely shred the leek, then cut the carrot into thin strips. Cut the snow peas into shreds and slice the ginger thinly into strips. Set aside some shredded leek, carrot, and ginger for the garnish.

3 Place the vegetables in a bowl and toss in the ginger wine and 1 tablespoon of the soy sauce.

4 Preheat the broiler to medium. Place the salmon fillets on a broiler rack and brush with the remaining soy sauce. Cook under the preheated hot broiler for 2–3 minutes on each side, or until cooked through. While the salmon is cooking, heat the vegetable oil in a preheated nonstick wok or large skillet and stir-fry the vegetables for 5 minutes, or until just tender. Take care that you do not overcook the vegetables—they should still have bite. Transfer to 4 serving plates. Drain the salmon on paper towels and serve on a bed of stir-fried vegetables. Garnish with the shredded leek, carrot, and ginger and serve.

fish balls in easy tomato sauce

 cook: 15 mins   prep: 15 mins   serves 4

White fish can often taste rather bland so, in this dish, fresh herbs and spices and a chunky tomato sauce give a burst of extra flavor to wake up the taste buds.

NUTRITIONAL INFORMATION	
Calories	134
Protein	22g
Carbohydrate	9g
Sugars	3g
Fat	1g
Saturates	0g

INGREDIENTS

few lengths of fresh chives
few sprigs of fresh dill
1 lb/450 g white fish fillets, skinned
salt and pepper
4 tbsp fresh whole-wheat
bread crumbs

SAUCE

2 oz/55 g white mushrooms, sliced
14 oz/400 g canned chopped tomatoes
½ tsp ground cinnamon
½ tsp ground cumin
1 tbsp lemon juice

cook's tip

Use whiting, haddock, ling, smoked haddock, or even smoked cod to make the fish balls. If you are making them for children, you can omit the spices.

1 Using a pair of kitchen scissors, snip the chives into short lengths, then snip the dill into small pieces. Set aside some herbs for the garnish. Check that there are no small bones remaining in the fish, removing any you find using tweezers. Season to taste with salt and pepper. Cut the fish into chunks and place in a food processor with the bread crumbs, chives, and dill. Process until the fish is finely chopped and the ingredients are mixed. Transfer to a bowl.

2 Take small pieces of the mixture and form into 16 walnut-size balls.

3 To make the sauce, chop the mushrooms into thin slices, then add to a pan with the tomatoes and their can juice. Stir in the ground cinnamon and cumin. Bring to a boil, then reduce the heat and let simmer. Add the fish balls and lemon juice, cover and cook over very low heat for 10 minutes. Transfer to a large serving dish, garnish with the reserved herbs, and serve immediately.

smoked haddock pie

serves 4   **prep: 15 mins** ⏲   **cook: 50 mins** ⏲

Real comfort food, fish pie is a family favorite and there is no reason to go without. Using skim milk and reduced fat cheese won't affect the flavor adversely, but will ensure a healthier meal.

INGREDIENTS

1 lb 10 oz/750 g mealy potatoes, cut into chunks

salt and pepper

1 lb/450 g smoked haddock fillets

2½ cups skim milk

4 juniper berries

4 black peppercorns

1 bay leaf

2 tbsp all-purpose flour

11½ oz/325 g canned corn, drained

2 tbsp butter

2 oz/55 g reduced fat Cheddar cheese, grated

fresh flatleaf parsley sprigs, to garnish

NUTRITIONAL INFORMATION

Calories 478

Protein 38g

Carbohydrate 69g

Sugars 17g

Fat 7g

Saturates 4g

variation

For a slightly different fish pie, try substituting smoked cod or whiting for the smoked haddock.

cook's tip

For the healthiest choice, look for naturally pale smoked haddock, rather than the bright yellow dyed fish, and canned corn with no added salt or sugar.

1 Preheat the oven to 400°F/200°C. Cook the potatoes in a large pan of lightly salted boiling water for 20 minutes, or until tender. Meanwhile, place the fish in a large skillet, pour in the milk and add the juniper berries, peppercorns, and bay leaf. Cover and let simmer over low heat for 10 minutes, or until the flesh flakes easily. Transfer the fish to a cutting board. Strain the milk and set aside. When the fish is cool enough to handle, remove and discard the skin and any small remaining bones. Flake the flesh and place in a bowl.

2 Place the flour in a pan and gradually whisk in 1¾ cups of the reserved milk, setting the rest aside. Bring to a boil over low heat, stirring, then let simmer for 1 minute. Season to taste with salt and pepper. Add the sauce to the fish with the corn, then spoon into an ovenproof dish.

3 When the potatoes are tender, drain well, then mash with the butter and remaining milk. Spoon the mash over the fish, spreading it out to cover. Sprinkle the cheese on top and bake in the oven for 25–30 minutes, or until golden. Serve immediately, garnished with parsley sprigs.

fish & yogurt quenelles

 cook: 15 mins

 prep: 15 mins, plus 30 mins chilling

serves 4

NUTRITIONAL INFORMATION

Calories	.228
Protein	.39g
Carbohydrate	.14g
Sugars	.7g
Fat	.2g
Saturates	.2g

These delicious quenelles, made from a thick purée of fish and yogurt, can be prepared well in advance and stored in the refrigerator before poaching.

INGREDIENTS

1 lb 10 oz/750 g white fish fillets, such as cod, coley, or whiting, skinned

2 small egg whites

½ tsp ground coriander

1 tsp ground mace

salt and pepper

⅔ cup lowfat plain yogurt

1 small onion, sliced

freshly cooked rice, to serve

SAUCE

1 bunch of watercress or arugula, trimmed

1¼ cups Chicken Stock (see page 11)

2 tbsp cornstarch

⅔ cup lowfat plain yogurt

2 tbsp lowfat sour cream

variation

Replace the cod fillets with salmon. Add grated lemon rind and chopped fresh dill to the processor with the spices, then proceed as in main recipe.

cook's tip

When poaching the quenelles, make sure that the water is just gently bubbling, otherwise the quenelles will break up.

1 Cut the fish into pieces, place it in a food processor and process for 30 seconds. Add the egg whites and process for an additional 30 seconds, or until the mixture forms a stiff paste. Add the ground coriander, mace, salt and pepper, and yogurt and process until smooth. Cover and let chill in the refrigerator for 30 minutes.

2 Spoon the mixture into a pastry bag and pipe into sausage shapes 4 inches/10 cm long. Alternatively, take rounded dessertspoons of the mixture and form into ovals, using 2 spoons.

3 Bring 2 inches/5 cm of water to a boil in a skillet and add the onion for flavoring. Lower the quenelles into the water, using a spatula or spoon. Cover, keep the water at a gentle boil and poach the quenelles for 8 minutes, turning them once. Remove with a slotted spoon and drain.

4 To make the sauce, coarsely chop the watercress, reserving a few sprigs for garnish, then place the remainder in a food processor, add the Chicken Stock and process until well blended. Pour into a pan. Stir the cornstarch into the yogurt and pour the mixture into the pan. Bring to a boil, stirring. Stir in the sour cream, season to taste, and remove from the heat. Garnish with the reserved watercress and serve with rice.

kedgeree

serves 4

prep: 15 mins, plus 10 mins cooling

cook: 40 mins

Derived from an Indian dish of rice, onions, lentils, and eggs, kedgeree dates from the days of the British Raj. Fish was added and kedgeree became a staple for leisurely colonial breakfasts.

INGREDIENTS

8 oz/225 g haddock fillet

8 oz/225 g smoked haddock fillet

1 tbsp corn oil

1 onion, chopped

½ tsp ground turmeric

½ tsp ground cumin

½ tsp chili powder

¼ tsp ground ginger

1 cup long-grain rice

salt and pepper

TO GARNISH

1 hard-cooked egg

2 tbsp chopped fresh parsley

NUTRITIONAL INFORMATION	
Calories	.340
Protein	.27g
Carbohydrate	.47g
Sugars	.1g
Fat	.5g
Saturates	.1g

variation

Traditionally, ⅔ cup light or sour cream is folded in with the fish. An alternative would be to use the same quantity of lowfat plain yogurt.

1 Place the haddock fillets in a large, heavy-bottom skillet. Pour in enough water to cover and poach gently over low heat for 10–15 minutes, or until the flesh flakes easily. Remove the fish with a spatula and let cool. Strain the cooking liquid into a measuring cup and make up to 2½ cups, if necessary.

2 Heat the oil in an ovenproof casserole. Add the onion and cook over low heat for 3 minutes, or until soft. Stir in the spices, then the rice, and cook, stirring, until well coated. Stir in the reserved cooking liquid. Bring to a boil, cover, and cook over low heat for 20 minutes, or until all the liquid has been absorbed and the rice is tender.

3 Meanwhile, skin the fish and remove any remaining bones. Flake the flesh. Fold the fish into the rice, season to taste with salt and pepper, and transfer to a large, warmed serving dish. Shell the hard-cooked egg and cut into quarters, then use to garnish the kedgeree. Sprinkle with chopped fresh parsley and serve immediately.

indian chili fish

cook: 10–20 mins

**prep: 10 mins,
plus 30 mins marinating**

serves 4

*The lime juice in this Indian-style recipe helps protect the delicate
flesh of the fish from the fierce heat of the broiler during cooking.
However, keep an eye open and lower the heat if it seems too dry.*

NUTRITIONAL INFORMATION	
Calories	144
Protein	21g
Carbohydrate	3g
Sugars	3g
Fat	5g
Saturates	1g

INGREDIENTS

½-inch/1-cm piece fresh gingerroot

4 flounder fillets, 4 oz/115 g each

1 tbsp peanut or corn oil

1 tbsp chopped fresh cilantro

2 tbsp lime juice

1¼ cups water

2 tbsp tomato paste

1 tbsp chili sauce

1 tbsp white wine vinegar

1 tsp brown sugar

fresh cilantro sprigs, to garnish

lime wedges, to serve

variation

This sauce is delicious with
shrimp. Add 1 lb/450 g
cooked, shelled shrimp to
the sauce to heat through
during the last 2–3 minutes
of cooking.

1 Grate the ginger and
set aside. Place the fish
in a shallow, nonmetallic dish.
Pour in the peanut oil,
chopped cilantro and lime juice
and turn the fish to coat well.
Cover with plastic wrap and let
marinate in the refrigerator for
30 minutes.

2 Preheat the broiler to
medium. Put the water,
tomato paste, chili sauce,
vinegar, grated ginger, and
sugar in a small pan. Bring to
a boil over low heat, stirring.
Let simmer, stirring
occasionally, for 5–8 minutes,
or until thickened.

3 Meanwhile, remove the
fish from the marinade
and cook under the broiler for
5–8 minutes, or until the flesh
is opaque and flakes easily.
Transfer to 4 serving plates and
spoon over the sauce. Garnish
with cilantro sprigs and serve
with lime wedges.

green fish curry

serves 4   **prep: 5 mins** ⏱   **cook: 20 mins** ⏱

This dish has a wonderful fresh, hot, exotic taste resulting from the generous amount of fresh herbs, sharp fresh chiles, and coconut milk. Serve immediately with freshly cooked basmati rice.

INGREDIENTS

1 tbsp vegetable oil	1 tbsp snipped fresh chives
2 scallions, sliced	⅔ cup coconut milk
1 tsp cumin seeds, ground	salt and pepper
2 fresh green chiles, chopped	4 white fish fillets, about
1 tsp coriander seeds, ground	8 oz/225 g each
4 tbsp chopped fresh cilantro	fresh mint sprigs, to garnish
4 tbsp chopped fresh mint	freshly cooked basmati rice, to serve

NUTRITIONAL INFORMATION

Calories	.223
Protein	.44g
Carbohydrate	.2g
Sugars	.2g
Fat	.5g
Saturates	.2g

variation

Choose cod or whiting for this dish and just use 1 fresh green chile, seeded and chopped if you don't like it too spicy.

cook's tip

Never overcook fish—it is surprising how little time it takes compared to meat. It will continue to cook while keeping warm in the oven and while being served at the table.

1 Heat the vegetable oil in a large, heavy-bottom skillet, add the scallions and stir-fry over medium heat for 2 minutes, or until softened but not colored. Stir in the ground cumin, chiles, and ground coriander and cook until the spices are fragrant.

2 Add the fresh cilantro, mint, chives, and coconut milk and season liberally with salt and pepper.

3 Using a spatula, carefully place the fish in the skillet and poach for 10–15 minutes, or until the flesh flakes easily when tested with a fork. Transfer the fish to 4 large, warmed serving plates, garnish with fresh mint sprigs, and serve immediately with freshly cooked basmati rice.

louisiana gumbo

serves 6   **prep: 20 mins** ⏲   **cook: 35 mins** ⏲

Transport yourself and your guests to Louisiana with this fabulous fish stew. There is an almost infinite number of recipes for this traditional dish, but they are all thickened with okra, a small green seed pod with a sticky juice that gives the stew a silky finish.

INGREDIENTS

2 tbsp corn oil

6 oz/175 g okra, trimmed and cut into

1-inch/2.5-cm pieces

2 onions, very finely chopped

4 celery stalks, very finely chopped

1 garlic clove, finely chopped

2 tbsp all-purpose flour

½ tsp sugar

1 tsp ground cumin

salt and pepper

3 cups Fish Stock

(see page 11)

1 red bell pepper, seeded and chopped

1 green bell pepper, seeded

and chopped

2 large tomatoes

12 oz/350 g large raw shrimp

4 tbsp chopped fresh parsley

1 tbsp chopped fresh cilantro

dash of Tabasco sauce

12 oz/350 g cod fillet, skinned

and cut into 1-inch/2.5-cm cubes

12 oz/350 g angler fish fillet, cut

into 1-inch/2.5-cm cubes

NUTRITIONAL INFORMATION

Calories 240
Protein 35g
Carbohydrate 12g
Sugars 6g
Fat 6g
Saturates 1g

variation

For a filé gumbo, add 1 teaspoon filé powder with the flour in Step 1 to thicken and flavor the stew. (Filé powder is made from sassafras leaves.)

cook's tip

To shell and devein shrimp, remove the head and tail, then peel away the shell. Using a sharp knife, cut along the back of the shrimp to remove the black intestinal thread that runs down the center. Wash well.

1 Heat half the oil in a large, ovenproof casserole. Add the okra and cook over low heat, stirring frequently, for 5 minutes, or until browned. Remove from the casserole and set aside. Add the remaining oil and the onion and celery and cook, stirring occasionally, for 5 minutes, or until softened. Add the garlic and cook for

1 minute. Stir in the flour, sugar, and cumin and season to taste with salt and pepper. Cook, stirring, for 2 minutes, then gradually stir in the Fish Stock and bring to a boil, stirring constantly.

2 Return the reserved okra to the casserole and add the bell peppers and tomatoes. Partially cover,

reduce the heat to very low, and let simmer gently, stirring occasionally, for 10 minutes. Shell and devein the shrimp (see Cook's Tip) and set aside.

3 Add the parsley and cilantro and Tabasco sauce to taste, then gently stir in the fish and shelled shrimp Cover and let simmer gently for 5 minutes, or until the fish

is cooked through and the shrimp have changed color. Transfer to a large, warmed serving dish and serve.

sole & smoked salmon rolls

serves 4   **prep: 30 mins** ⟳   **cook: 20 mins** ⟳

In this elegant dish, the delicate flavor of sole and smoked salmon blend together perfectly with a light citrus filling. Served with steamed vegetables, such as broccoli, it is ideal for a dinner party.

INGREDIENTS

1 cup fresh whole-wheat bread crumbs

½ tsp grated lime rind

1 tbsp lime juice

¼ cup lowfat soft cheese

salt and pepper

4 sole fillets, about 4½ oz/125 g each

2 oz/55 g smoked salmon

⅔ cup Fish Stock

(see page 11)

⅔ cup lowfat plain yogurt

1 tbsp chopped fresh chervil

fresh chervil sprigs, to garnish

TO SERVE

selection of freshly steamed vegetables

lime wedges

NUTRITIONAL INFORMATION

Calories 191

Protein 3g

Carbohydrate 9g

Sugars 3g

Fat 4g

Saturates 2g

variation

If fresh chervil is unavailable, replace it with fresh chives, parsley, or a few sprigs of fresh tarragon.

cook's tip

When buying fresh fish, choose fish with bright eyes and red gills. The fish should be firm to the touch, with just a very slight "fishy" smell.

1 Preheat the oven to 375°F/190°C. Mix the bread crumbs, lime rind and juice, soft cheese, and salt and pepper together in a bowl until a soft stuffing mixture is formed.

2 Skin the sole fillets by inserting a sharp knife in between the skin and flesh at the tail end. Holding the skin in your fingers and keeping it taut, strip the flesh away from the skin. Halve the sole fillets lengthwise.

3 Place strips of smoked salmon over the skinned side of each fillet. Trim the salmon as necessary. Spoon one-eighth of the stuffing onto each fish fillet and press down along the fish with the back of a spoon. Carefully roll up from the head to the tail end. Place, seam-side down, in a large ovenproof dish and pour in the Fish Stock.

4 Bake in the preheated oven for 15 minutes. Using a spatula, transfer the fish to a warmed serving plate, cover, and keep warm. Pour the cooking juices into a pan and add the yogurt and chopped fresh chervil. Season to taste with salt and pepper and heat gently without boiling. Garnish the fish rolls with chervil sprigs and serve with the yogurt sauce, steamed vegetables, and lime wedges.

halibut pockets

serves 4   **prep: 20 mins**   **cook: 10–15 mins**

Cooking in a pocket is an excellent lowfat technique that works especially well with fish, as it protects the delicate flesh. It is also a very attractive way to present a main meal.

INGREDIENTS

4 baby leeks, cut into thin strips

4 baby zucchinis, cut into thin sticks

4 baby carrots, cut into thin sticks

1 fennel bulb, halved and cut into thin strips

4oz/115 g chanterelle mushrooms, thinly sliced

2 tbsp finely chopped fresh chervil

salt and pepper

4 halibut steaks, about 6 oz/175 g each

4 tsp extra virgin olive oil

4 tbsp white wine

NUTRITIONAL INFORMATION	
Calories	234
Protein	33g
Carbohydrate	6g
Sugars	3g
Fat	8g
Saturates	1g

variation

Substitute 2 canned artichoke hearts, drained, for the fennel strips, and replace the halibut steaks with salmon steaks.

1 Preheat the oven to 375°F/190°C. Cut out 4 x 12-inch/30-cm squares of parchment paper and spread out on a counter.

2 Divide the leeks, zucchinis, carrots, fennel, and mushrooms equally between the paper squares. Sprinkle with half the chopped chervil and season to taste with salt and pepper. Top each bed of vegetables with a halibut steak and sprinkle with the remaining chopped herbs. Fold up the edges of the paper, but do not seal. Drizzle 1 teaspoon of olive oil and 1 tablespoon of white wine over each fish steak, then fold over the edges of the paper to seal and make a loosely wrapped pocket.

3 Place the pockets on a large baking sheet and bake in the preheated oven for 10–15 minutes, or until the pockets are puffed up. Transfer the pockets to 4 large, warmed serving plates and serve immediately.

baked lemon sole

cook: 15 mins   **prep: 5 mins**   **serves 4**

A simple mixture of herbs, lemon juice, and garlic is delicious, but will not overwhelm the delicate flavor of the fish. Serve with freshly cooked rice and vegetables for a filling supper.

NUTRITIONAL INFORMATION	
Calories	193
Protein	30g
Carbohydrate	0g
Sugars	0g
Fat	8g
Saturates	1g

INGREDIENTS

2 garlic cloves

4 lemon sole fillets,
about 6 oz/175 g each

1 shallot, finely chopped

2 fresh lemon thyme sprigs, plus
extra to garnish

2 fresh lemon balm sprigs, plus
extra to garnish

salt and pepper

grated rind and juice of 1 lemon

2 tbsp extra virgin olive oil

cook's tip

Lemon sole is not related to Dover sole and is less expensive, but still has a fine flavor and delicate flesh. It is available from most large supermarkets.

1 Preheat the oven to 350°F/180°C. Using a sharp knife, thinly slice the garlic and set aside.

2 Arrange the sole fillets in a single layer in the bottom of a large ovenproof dish and sprinkle with the shallot. Place the reserved garlic slices and fresh herb sprigs on top of the fillets and season to taste with salt and pepper. Mix the lemon juice and olive oil together in a small measuring cup and pour it over the fish.

3 Bake in the preheated oven for 15 minutes, or until the fish flakes easily when tested with a fork.

Sprinkle with lemon rind, garnish with the extra fresh herbs, and serve immediately.

sole paupiettes

serves 4   **prep: 10 mins** ⏲   **cook: 45 mins** ⏲

This delicate dish of sole fillets rolled up with spinach and shrimp, then served in a creamy ginger sauce will be an instant favorite with both family and friends.

INGREDIENTS

generous 2¾ cups young spinach leaves	2 thin slices fresh gingerroot, chopped
2 lemon soles, filleted	⅔ cup Fish Stock (see page 11) or water
salt and pepper	2 tsp cornstarch
4½ oz/125 g cooked shelled shrimp, thawed if frozen	4 tbsp light cream
	6 tbsp lowfat plain yogurt
2 tsp corn oil	whole cooked shrimp, to garnish
2–4 scallions, finely sliced	

NUTRITIONAL INFORMATION	
Calories	253
Protein	24g
Carbohydrate	9g
Sugars	7g
Fat	14g
Saturates	2g

variation

Replace the lemon sole fillets with flounder fillets and substitute twists of lemon for the cooked shrimp.

cook's tip

If using frozen shrimp, make sure that they are completely thawed out before cooking. Keep the shrimp covered in the refrigerator until ready to use and always use on the same day as thawed.

1 Trim the stalks from the spinach and discard. Rinse the leaves under cold running water and pat dry on paper towels. Season the fish with salt and pepper, then divide the spinach between the seasoned fish fillets, laying the leaves on the skin side. Divide half the shrimp between them. Roll up the fillets from head to tail and secure with wooden toothpicks. Arrange the rolls on a plate in the bottom of a large bamboo steamer.

2 Stand a low metal trivet in the wok and add enough water to come almost to the top of it. Bring to a boil. Place the bamboo steamer on the trivet, cover with the steamer lid, then the wok lid, or cover with a domed piece of foil. Steam gently for 30 minutes, or until the fish is tender and cooked through.

3 Remove the fish rolls and keep warm. Empty the wok and wipe dry with paper towels. Heat the oil in the wok until hot. Add the scallions and ginger and stir-fry for 1–2 minutes.

4 Add the Fish Stock to the wok and bring to a boil. Blend the cornstarch with the cream. Add the yogurt and remaining shrimp to the wok and heat until boiling. Add a little sauce to the blended cream and return it all to the wok. Heat until thickened. Season to taste. Serve the paupiettes with the sauce and garnished with whole shrimp.

caribbean snapper

serves 4　　　**prep: 15 mins, plus 30 mins marinating**　　　**cook: 20 mins**

Snapper is actually a large family of fish that range in color from pink, through red, to orange. It is much prized in the Caribbean for its delicate flavor. Serve with corn bread for a complete meal.

INGREDIENTS

2 tbsp dark rum	2 tsp tomato paste
¼ cup white wine	1 red bell pepper, seeded and
1 tbsp finely chopped fresh gingerroot	coarsely chopped
1 garlic clove, finely chopped	scant 2½ cups Fish Stock
salt and pepper	(see page 11)
1 lb 2 oz/500 g red snapper fillets	2 large tomatoes, peeled, seeded, and
1 onion	coarsely chopped
1 tbsp corn oil	1 mango, peeled, seeded, and
2 tbsp all-purpose flour	coarsely chopped

NUTRITIONAL INFORMATION

Calories	255
Protein	. . . . .27g
Carbohydrate	. . . . .21g
Sugars	. . . . .12g
Fat	. . . . .5g
Saturates	. . . . .1g

variation

Add 5 oz/140 g canned corn, drained, and substitute 10 oz/280 g peeled diced pumpkin for the mango.

cook's tip

Don't skin the fish fillets before cooking as the pieces may fall apart. If red snapper is unavailable, then use pompano instead.

1 Mix the rum, wine, ginger, and garlic in a large, shallow, nonmetallic dish and season to taste with pepper. Cut the fish fillets into 1½-inch/4-cm pieces and add to the marinade. Using a spoon, carefully coat the fish with the marinade. Cover with plastic wrap and let marinate in the refrigerator for 30 minutes.

2 Remove the fish using a slotted spoon and set aside. Set aside the marinade. Using a sharp knife, cut the onion into wedges. Heat the oil in a large pan, add the onion wedges and cook over medium heat, stirring occasionally, for 5 minutes, or until just starting to brown. Stir in the flour and add the tomato paste and red bell pepper. Gradually stir in the Fish Stock and the reserved marinade and bring to a boil, stirring constantly. Reduce the heat and let simmer for 3 minutes.

3 Add the fish, tomatoes, and mango to the pan and season to taste with salt. Cover and let simmer for 8 minutes, or until the fish flakes easily, then serve.

cajun-spiced fish

serves 4   **prep: 5 mins** ⏲   **cook: 10 mins** ⏲

Descended from immigrant French cuisine, Cajun cooking is marked with a practical approach that makes the most of the locally available ingredients in the countryside round New Orleans.

INGREDIENTS

1 tbsp lime juice

2 tbsp lowfat plain yogurt

4 swordfish steaks,
about 6 oz/175 g each

corn oil, for brushing

lemon wedges, to serve

SPICE MIX

1 tsp paprika

1 tsp cayenne pepper

1 tsp ground cumin

1 tsp mustard powder

1 tsp dried oregano

NUTRITIONAL INFORMATION	
Calories 215	
Protein 33g	
Carbohydrate 2g	
Sugars 2g	
Fat 8g	
Saturates 2g	

cook's tip

Brush the fish steaks lightly with oil and cook under a preheated hot broiler or on a lit barbecue instead. Brush again with oil when you turn them over.

1 First make the spice mix by blending all the ingredients in a bowl. Mix the lime juice and yogurt in a separate bowl.

2 Pat the fish steaks dry with paper towels, then brush both sides with the yogurt mixture. Use your hands to coat both sides of the fish with the spice mix, rubbing it well into the flesh.

3 Brush a grill pan with a little corn oil. Add the fish steaks and cook for 5 minutes over medium heat, then turn over and cook for an additional 4 minutes, or until the flesh flakes easily when tested with a fork. Serve straight from the pan with lemon wedges.

sea trout in a salt crust

⏱ **cook: 25 mins**   ⏲ **prep: 20 mins, plus 10 mins standing**   **serves 4**

This is an unusual, but very effective, way to cook fish, sealing in all the delicate flavor of the sea trout. When you are ready to serve, simply break the crust and lift out the perfectly baked fish.

NUTRITIONAL INFORMATION	
Calories 282	
Protein 49g	
Carbohydrate 0g	
Sugars 2g	
Fat 9g	
Saturates 2g	

INGREDIENTS

about 4 lb 8 oz/2 kg coarse sea salt

1 tsp dried thyme

1 tsp dried rosemary

1 tsp dried dill

3 garlic cloves, very finely chopped

1 large egg white

4 whole sea trout, about 10½ oz/300 g each

salt and pepper

2 fresh thyme sprigs

2 fresh rosemary sprigs

2 fresh dill sprigs

1 Preheat the oven to 475°F/240°C. Mix the sea salt, dried herbs, garlic, and egg white together in a large bowl until all the salt crystals are moistened.

2 Using a sharp knife, slit the fish open along the belly and remove the innards. Rinse the fish inside and out under cold running water and pat dry with paper towels. Season the cavity with salt and pepper to taste and place the fresh herbs inside. Line a large ovenproof dish with a double layer of foil, leaving an overhang, and make a thick layer of the salt mixture on the bottom. Place the fish on top and cover with remaining salt. Bring up the edges of the foil to enclose the salt.

3 Bake in the preheated oven for 25 minutes. Turn off the heat, but do not remove the dish for an additional 10 minutes. To serve, carefully lift out the foil package, open up and break away all the salt crust, gently brushing off residual traces. Lift off the individual fish, transfer to 4 large serving plates and serve immediately.

cook's tip

Choose firm fish with bright eyes and bright pink gills, which indicate freshness. Buy the fish on the day you want to cook it. Fresh fish should be stored in the refrigerator and used within 12 hours.

bouillabaisse

serves 8   **prep: 30 mins, plus 🕒 30 mins marinating**   **cook: 20 mins 🕒**

This is probably the most famous fish stew in the world and just about every French village on the Mediterranean coastline has its own particular version. A good-quality fish stock is absolutely essential. Serve with plenty of French bread.

INGREDIENTS

2 lb 12 oz/1.25 kg sea bass, filleted, skinned, and cut into bite-size pieces

2 lb 12 oz/1.25 kg redfish, filleted, skinned, and cut into bite-size pieces

3 tbsp extra virgin olive oil

grated rind of 1 orange

1 garlic clove, finely chopped

pinch of saffron threads

2 tbsp pastis

1 lb/450 g live mussels

1 large cooked crab

1 small fennel bulb, finely chopped

2 celery stalks, finely chopped

1 onion, finely chopped

5 cups Fish Stock

(see page 11)

8 oz/225 g small new potatoes

8 oz/225 g tomatoes, peeled, seeded, and chopped

1 lb/450 g large raw shrimp

salt and pepper

NUTRITIONAL INFORMATION	
Calories	.359
Protein	.54g
Carbohydrate	.7g
Sugars	.2g
Fat	.13g
Saturates	.1g

variation

Replace the sea bass with whiting and substitute clams for the mussels. You could also add cooked shelled shrimp and garnish with whole cooked ones.

cook's tip

Redfish is a member of the drum family. It is a traditional ingredient in bouillabaisse, but if you cannot find it, use red snapper instead.

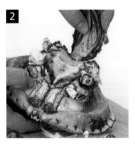

1 Put the fish pieces in a large bowl and add 2 tablespoons of the olive oil, the orange rind, garlic, saffron, and pastis. Turn the fish pieces to coat well, cover, and let marinate in the refrigerator for 30 minutes.

2 Meanwhile, clean the mussels by scrubbing or scraping the shells and pulling out any beards that are attached to them. Remove the meat from the cooked crab and chop. Set aside.

3 Heat the remaining olive oil in a large ovenproof casserole. Add the fennel, celery, and onion and cook over low heat, stirring occasionally, for 5 minutes, or until softened. Add the Fish Stock and bring to a boil. Add the new potatoes and tomatoes and cook over medium heat for 7 minutes.

4 Reduce the heat and add the fish, starting with the thickest chunks. Discard any mussels that do not close when sharply tapped with the back of a knife and add the remainder to the stew.

Add the shrimp and pieces of crab and let simmer until the fish is opaque, the mussels have opened again and the shrimp have changed color. Discard any mussels that remain closed. Season the bouillabaisse to taste with salt and pepper and serve.

mussels in white wine

Also known as moules marinière, this quick and simple dish is the perfect way to serve seaside-fresh mussels. However, do not gather them yourself, as they may be toxic from pollution in the sea.

INGREDIENTS

4 shallots

3 garlic cloves

2 tbsp butter

1¼ cups dry white wine

1 bouquet garni

salt and pepper

4½ lb/2 kg live mussels, scrubbed and debearded

2 tbsp chopped fresh parsley

NUTRITIONAL INFORMATION

Calories	.236
Protein	.27g
Carbohydrate	.3g
Sugars	.2g
Fat	.8g
Saturates	.4g

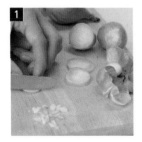  

variation

For moules marinière Normandy-style, substitute a good-quality hard cider for the wine. Replace the bouquet garni with sprigs of thyme and a bay leaf.

1 Using a sharp knife, chop the shallots finely, then crush the garlic. Set aside. Discard any mussels with broken shells, or any that refuse to close when tapped with a knife.

2 Melt the butter in a large pan. Add the shallots and garlic and cook over low heat, stirring frequently, for 5 minutes, or until softened. Pour in the wine, add the bouquet garni and season to taste with salt and pepper. Bring to a boil over medium heat and add the mussels. Cover and cook, shaking the pan frequently, for 5 minutes, or until the mussels have opened. Discard any mussels that remain closed.

3 Remove and discard the bouquet garni. Using a slotted spoon, divide the mussels between 4 soup bowls. Tilt the pan and spoon a little of the cooking liquid over each plate. Sprinkle with the chopped fresh parsley and serve immediately.

spaghetti with saffron mussels

🕐 **cook: 25 mins**   ⏲ **prep: 20 mins**   **serves 4**

This is a pasta dish with attitude—its elegant color and sophisticated flavor put it in a class of its own, yet it is quick and easy to make, as well as a healthy and filling supper dish.

NUTRITIONAL INFORMATION	
Calories	479
Protein	. . . . .23g
Carbohydrate	. . . . .76g
Sugars	. . . . .6g
Fat	. . . . .6g
Saturates	. . . . .1g

INGREDIENTS

¼ tsp saffron threads

¾ cup water

2 lb/900 g live mussels, scrubbed
and debearded

½ cup white wine

1 tbsp corn oil

1 small onion, finely chopped

2 tbsp all-purpose flour

⅔ cup Noilly Prat or other
extra dry vermouth

12 oz/350 g dried spaghetti

2 tbsp snipped fresh dill

salt and pepper

cook's tip

To prepare mussels, scrub under cold running water and scrape off all barnacles with a sharp knife. Tug off the beards. Discard any with broken shells and any that do not shut when tapped with a knife.

1 Gently crush the saffron threads and place in a bowl with the water. Let soak. Discard any mussels that do not close when sharply tapped with a knife, and put the remainder in a large pan. Add the wine and bring to a boil. Cover and cook over high heat, shaking the pan occasionally, for 5 minutes, or until the mussels have opened.

Remove the mussels with a slotted spoon, discarding any that remain closed. Strain the cooking liquid through a cheesecloth-lined strainer and set aside. When the mussels are cool enough to handle, remove from their shells.

2 Heat the oil in a heavy-bottom skillet. Add the onion and cook over low heat for 5 minutes, or until soft. Stir in the flour and cook, stirring, for 1 minute. Remove from the heat and add the vermouth and the soaking liquid, whisking constantly. Return to low heat and cook for 2 minutes, until thickened.

3 Cook the pasta in a large pan of lightly salted boiling water for 8–10 minutes, until tender but firm to the bite. Meanwhile, place 4 tablespoons of the reserved cooking liquid in a pan and stir in the saffron mixture. Add the mussels and dill and season to taste with salt and pepper. Cook over low heat until heated through. Drain the spaghetti, place in a large serving bowl and toss with the sauce. Serve immediately.

fish & seafood chowder

serves 4 **prep: 20 mins, plus 10 mins cooling** ⏲ **cook: 25 mins** ⏲

Served with plenty of warm crusty bread and a fresh, crisp salad, this tasty soup makes a substantial lunch or supper dish for any occasion, whether it is for family or friends.

INGREDIENTS

2 lb 4 oz/1 kg live mussels

1 large onion, thinly sliced

2 garlic cloves, chopped

3 bay leaves

few sprigs of fresh parsley

few sprigs of fresh thyme

1¼ cups water

8 oz/225 g smoked haddock fillets

1 lb 2 oz/500 g potatoes, peeled and diced

4 celery stalks, thickly sliced

2½ cups water

9 oz/250 g canned corn kernels, drained and rinsed

⅔ cup lowfat plain yogurt

1 tsp cornstarch

⅔ cup dry white wine, or hard cider

½ tsp cayenne pepper, or to taste

salt and pepper

2 tbsp chopped fresh parsley

warm crusty bread, to serve

NUTRITIONAL INFORMATION

Calories	.286
Protein	.30g
Carbohydrate	.31g
Sugars	.6g
Fat	.3g
Saturates	.2g

variation

Different combinations of fish and shellfish would also work. Try using clams, smoked cod fillets, or whiting.

cook's tip

When buying mussels, always choose those with undamaged shells and those that have a fresh, salty smell. Discard all those that feel heavy or light, or loose as they may be dead.

1 Scrub the mussels, pull off any beards that are attached to them, then rinse thoroughly. Discard any mussels that do not close when sharply tapped with the back of a knife.

2 Place the onion, garlic, herbs, water, and mussels in a large pan. Cover and cook over high heat, shaking the pan occasionally, for 5 minutes, or until the mussels have opened.

3 Line a strainer with cheesecloth and strain the mussels and liquid into a bowl. When the mussels are cool enough to handle, remove from their shells. Discard any mussels that are closed. Set aside the liquid.

4 Place the haddock and vegetables in a large pan, add the water, cover, and let simmer for 10 minutes. Remove the fish, then skin, bone and flake it. Strain the cooking liquid into the seafood liquid and set aside the vegetables. Return the cooking liquid to the rinsed-out pan, add the corn and bring to a boil.

5 Stir the yogurt and cornstarch together, then stir in a little of the fish liquid. Pour it into the pan and stir well then add the reserved fish and vegetables. Add the wine, season with cayenne and pepper and heat the soup gently. Season to taste and transfer to a serving plate. Sprinkle with the parsley and serve with crusty bread.

shellfish stew

serves 8   **prep: 20 mins** ☾   **cook: 20 mins** 🍲

This is an ideal dish for an informal supper party, as it looks and tastes spectacular, yet is easy to make. Provide several empty dishes for collecting the shells, and bread for mopping up the juices.

INGREDIENTS

24 live mussels

24 clams

1 lb/450 g sea bream fillets

generous 5 cups Fish Stock (see page 11)

1 cup dry white wine

2 shallots, finely chopped

24 raw Mediterranean shrimp, shelled and deveined

1 lb 9 oz/700 g tomatoes, peeled, seeded, and coarsely chopped

3 tbsp snipped fresh chives

grated rind of 1 lemon

pinch of saffron threads

3 tbsp finely chopped fresh parsley

salt and pepper

NUTRITIONAL INFORMATION	
Calories	157
Protein	. . . . .23g
Carbohydrate	. . . . .5g
Sugars	. . . . .3g
Fat	. . . . .3g
Saturates	. . . . .0g

variation

Sea bass would also work very well in this stew. If you cannot find the Mediterranean shrimp, use ordinary shrimp instead.

cook's tip

This dish is quite messy, so provide finger bowls filled with hot water and a slice of lemon so each guest can wash their fingers after eating.

1 Clean the mussels by scrubbing and scraping the shells and pulling out any beards that are attached to them. Discard any with broken shells, or that do not close when sharply tapped with a knife. Scrub the clams and discard any that do not close when tapped. Cut the sea bream into bite-size pieces and set aside.

2 Pour the Fish Stock and wine into a large, heavy-bottom pan and bring to a boil. Add the mussels, clams ,and shallots, cover and cook over medium heat for 4 minutes.

3 Strain the shellfish, reserving the stock. Discard any mussels or clams that remain closed and set the remainder aside. Rinse the pan and strain the stock back into it through a cheesecloth-lined strainer. Bring back to a boil and add the shrimp and sea bream. Stir in the tomatoes, chives, lemon rind, saffron, and parsley, and season to taste. Cook over low heat for 10 minutes, or until the fish flakes easily when tested with the tip of a knife.

4 Remove the pan from the heat, add the mussels and clams, cover, and let stand for 5 minutes. Divide the stew between 4 soup plates and serve.

rigatoni with squid

serves 4   **prep: 10 mins**   **cook: 50–55 mins**

This delicious combination of pasta and squid is excellent for a light summer supper. If time is limited, use fresh pasta, as it takes less time to cook than dried. Farfalle and penne would also work well.

INGREDIENTS

1 red bell pepper	14 oz/400 g canned chopped tomatoes
1 yellow bell pepper	½–1 tsp chili powder
1 tbsp corn oil	9 oz/250 g dried rigatoni
12 oz/350 g prepared squid rings	2 tbsp chopped fresh basil
1 onion, chopped	salt and pepper
1 garlic clove, finely chopped	

NUTRITIONAL INFORMATION

Calories	.349
Protein	.23g
Carbohydrate	.56g
Sugars	.10g
Fat	.5g
Saturates	.0g

variation

Use fresh tomatoes instead of canned when they are in season. Peel, seed, and chop 1 lb 10 oz/750 g tomatoes and add them in Step 2.

cook's tip

The trick with squid is to cook it very rapidly. It is only tough and rubbery when it is over-cooked. If stir-frying, cook the squid for 2 minutes, until the rings are opaque.

1 Preheat the broiler to medium. Place the bell peppers on a baking sheet and roast under the broiler, turning frequently, for 15 minutes, or until charred and starting to blacken. Remove with tongs, place in a plastic bag and seal the top. When the bell peppers are cool enough to handle, rub off the skins, seed, and chop the flesh.

2 Heat the oil in a heavy-bottom skillet. Add the squid rings and stir-fry for 1–2 minutes, or until opaque. Remove the squid and set aside. Add the onion and garlic and cook for 5 minutes, or until soft. Add the tomatoes, bell peppers, and chili powder to taste, reduce the heat, and let simmer for 20–25 minutes, or until thickened.

3 Meanwhile, cook the pasta in a pan of lightly salted water for 8–10 minutes, or until tender but still firm to the bite. Just before serving, stir the squid rings and basil into the sauce and season to taste with salt and pepper. Heat through for 2–3 minutes. Drain the pasta, transfer to a serving dish and toss with the sauce. Serve.

shrimp stir-fry

serves 4   **prep: 5 mins** ◔   **cook: 8 mins** ◔

This colorful dish takes hardly any time to prepare and cook, which makes it an ideal midweek supper. Serve with plain boiled rice or with freshly cooked noodles.

INGREDIENTS

8 scallions

1 green bell pepper

1 red bell pepper

2 tbsp peanut or corn oil

2 garlic cloves, very finely chopped

1 tbsp grated fresh gingerroot

1¾ cups snow peas

1 lb/450 g raw jumbo shrimp, thawed if frozen, shelled, and deveined

4 tbsp Chinese rice wine

NUTRITIONAL INFORMATION

Calories 203

Protein 28g

Carbohydrate 5g

Sugars 4g

Fat 8g

Saturates 1g

variation

Substitute thinly sliced broccoli florets for the snow peas for an equally colorful and tasty dish. Replace the Chinese rice wine with dry sherry.

1   Using a sharp knife, trim the scallions and finely chop. Deseed and slice the bell peppers.

2   Heat the peanut oil in a preheated wok or heavy-bottom skillet. Add the scallions, garlic, ginger, and bell peppers, and stir-fry over medium–high heat for 4 minutes.

3   Add the snow peas and shrimp and stir-fry for 4 minutes, or until the shrimp have changed color. Stir in the Chinese rice wine, then transfer to 4 large, warmed serving plates and serve.

mexican shrimp

⏱ **cook: 20 mins**   ⏱ **prep: 5 mins**   **serves 4**

For a very special treat, you could use large or jumbo shrimp for this tasty dish. If the shrimp are frozen, make sure that they are fully thawed out before you start cooking.

NUTRITIONAL INFORMATION	
Calories	189
Protein	27g
Carbohydrate	9g
Sugars	7g
Fat	5g
Saturates	1g

INGREDIENTS

1 fresh green chile

1 tbsp corn oil

1 large onion, finely chopped

3 garlic cloves, finely chopped

3 beefsteak tomatoes, peeled, seeded, and chopped

1 bay leaf

1 lb/450 g cooked, shelled shrimp

1 tbsp lime juice

few sprigs of fresh cilantro, plus extra to garnish

salt and pepper

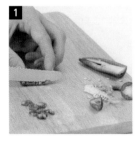

cook's tip

It is difficult to estimate how hot chiles are unless you know the variety, and even then, individual specimens may vary. Dark green chiles are usually hotter than pale green ones.

1 Using a sharp knife, cut the chile in half and remove and discard the seeds, then chop finely and set aside.

2 Heat the corn oil in a heavy-bottom skillet. Add the onion and garlic and cook over low heat, stirring occasionally, for 5 minutes, or until softened.

3 Add the chopped tomatoes, reserved chile, and bay leaf and let simmer over low heat, stirring occasionally, for 10 minutes, or until thickened.

4 Toss the shrimp in the lime juice and stir into the sauce. Chop the cilantro and stir into the sauce. Season to taste with salt and pepper. Cook for an additional 4 minutes, or until heated through. Transfer to 4 large serving bowls and garnish with fresh cilantro sprigs. Serve immediately.

hot & spicy shrimp

serves 4   **prep: 20 mins** ⏱   **cook: 15 mins** ♨

This is a fiery dish for lovers of chile—so beware. You can reduce the number of chiles if you prefer a milder flavoring. Shrimp paste is available from Chinese food stores and large supermarkets.

INGREDIENTS

1 garlic clove

½-inch/1-cm cube shrimp paste

½-inch/1-cm piece fresh gingerroot, thinly sliced

4 fresh red chiles, seeded and finely chopped

1 tbsp peanut or corn oil

4 scallions, chopped

1 green bell pepper, seeded and cut into thin sticks

14 oz/400 g canned chopped tomatoes

1 tbsp brown sugar

¼ cup water (optional)

12 oz/350 g cooked, shelled shrimp

3–4 scallions, to garnish

NUTRITIONAL INFORMATION

Calories 165	
Protein 22g	
Carbohydrate 10g	
Sugars 10g	
Fat 5g	
Saturates 1g	

variation

This sauce is also delicious with crab. Use 2 cooked crabs, weighing about 1 lb 7 oz/650 g. Remove the meat and add it in Step 3. Proceed as in recipe.

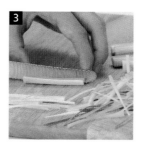

cook's tip

If you prepare the scallions for the garnish before cooking, then place the shreds in a bowl of ice water to keep them fresh.

1 Peel and finely chop the garlic, then put it in a mortar with the shrimp paste, ginger, and chiles. Using a pestle, grind to a paste. Heat the peanut oil in a preheated wok or large, heavy-bottom skillet and cook the spice paste over medium heat, stirring constantly, for 1 minute. Do not let it brown.

2 Add the scallions and green bell pepper and cook, stirring constantly, for 5 minutes, then stir in the tomatoes and sugar. Bring to a boil, stirring constantly. If the sauce is too thick, add the water. Reduce the heat and let simmer for 5 minutes.

3 Stir in the shrimp and cook for 4 minutes, or until heated through. Using a sharp knife, finely shred the scallions for the garnish. Transfer the shrimp to 4 large serving bowls, garnish with the shredded scallions and serve immediately.

seafood pizza

serves 4 **prep: 25 mins, plus 1 hr rising** **cook: 55 mins**

Make a change from the standard pizza toppings—this dish is piled high with seafood and baked with a delicious broiled red bell pepper and tomato sauce. Serve with a crisp salad for a delicious light lunch.

INGREDIENTS

5 oz/140 g standard pizza base mix

4 tbsp chopped fresh dill or 2 tbsp dried dill

fresh dill, to garnish

SAUCE

1 large red bell pepper

14 oz/400 g canned chopped tomatoes with onion and herbs

3 tbsp tomato paste

salt and pepper

TOPPING

12 oz/350 g assorted cooked seafood, thawed if frozen

1 tbsp capers in brine, drained

2 tbsp pitted black olives in brine, drained

1 oz/25 g lowfat mozzarella cheese, grated

1 tbsp freshly grated Parmesan cheese

NUTRITIONAL INFORMATION	
Calories	248
Protein	27g
Carbohydrate	22g
Sugars	7g
Fat	6g
Saturates	20g

variation

If you cannot find canned tomatoes with onions and herbs, add 1 chopped onion and 1 teaspoon of mixed dried herbs with the tomatoes in Step 3.

cook's tip

The easiest way to peel off bell pepper skins is to place the bell peppers under a hot broiler until the skins are blackened and blistered, then place in a plastic bag. Let cool, then peel the skins off.

1 Place the pizza base mix in a large bowl and stir in the dill. Make the dough according to the package instructions.

2 Press the dough into a circle measuring 10 inches/25 cm across on a baking sheet lined with parchment paper. Let rise for 1 hour until doubled in size.

3 Preheat the oven to 400°F/200°C. Preheat the broiler to hot. To make the sauce, halve and seed the bell pepper and arrange on a broiler rack. Cook under the preheated hot broiler for 8–10 minutes, or until the flesh is soft and the skin is blackened and blistered. Let cool slightly, then peel off the skin, chop the flesh, and place in a pan with the tomatoes. Bring to a boil and let simmer for 10 minutes. Stir in the tomato paste and season to taste with salt and pepper.

4 Spread the sauce over the pizza base and top with the seafood. Sprinkle over the capers and olives, top with the cheeses, and bake in the preheated oven for 25–30 minutes. Garnish with sprigs of dill and serve hot, cut into slices.

desserts & baking

For many people, a meal is not complete without a dessert, but they mistakenly believe that they must forego that pleasure when following a low fat eating plan. For such people, this chapter will be a revelation. Treats for those with a sweet tooth include Hot Chocolate Cherries (see page 220), Banana Soufflés (see page 222), and Magic Cheesecake (see page 237). There are familiar delights, such as Stuffed Baked Apples (see page 219), and more unusual temptations, such as Indonesian Black Rice Pudding (see page 236). Fruit features in many guises, from simple Charbroiled Fruit (see page 214) to a pretty Fig & Watermelon Salad (see page 218). For summer time, there is a selection of refreshing ice desserts with a fraction of the fat found in traditional ice cream. Try Coffee Ice Cream (see page 228) to round off a dinner party, or Peach Sherbet (see page 230) after an alfresco lunch.

Home-baked cakes and cookies are always popular, but they don't have to involve lots of butter. If you still need convincing, just look at the wonderful Fat Free Marble Cake (see page 248) with its decorative chocolate and vanilla patterning. As its name suggests, it contains no fat at all. Other delicious low fat confections include a marvelously moist and light Apricot Cake (see page 244) and Fruity Oat Crunch Bars (see page 253), both destined to become a firm family favorite.

charbroiled fruit

serves 4 **prep: 20 mins** **cook: 10 mins**

Fruit is the obvious choice for a lowfat dessert, but it can be rather unexciting. Liven it up with a flavorsome glaze and serve hot with lowfat plain yogurt or fat free mascarpone cheese.

INGREDIENTS

1 pineapple	1-inch/2.5-cm piece fresh
1 papaya	gingerroot, grated
1 mango	4 kiwifruit, peeled and sliced
6 tbsp honey	2 nectarines, peeled, pitted,
grated rind of 1 orange	and halved
grated rind of 1 lemon	2 bananas, peeled and halved

NUTRITIONAL INFORMATION

Calories	320
Protein	. . . . .4g
Carbohydrate	. . . . .79g
Sugars	. . . . .78g
Fat	. . . . .1g
Saturates	. . . . .0g

variation

Other fruits that are delicious cooked in the same way include peaches, apples, and pears. They all cook equally well on a barbecue.

cook's tip

Use a single flower honey, if possible. Try clover, acacia, orange blossom, or lavender—they will impart a delicious flavor to the broiled fruit.

1 Preheat the broiler to medium. Using a sharp knife, cut the plume off the pineapple and discard. Stand the pineapple upright and slice off the skin. Remove any eyes and slice into rings. Set 4 rings aside and store the rest in the refrigerator for another day.

2 Cut the papaya in half and scoop out the seeds with a metal spoon. Peel and slice. Set aside 4 slices and store the rest in the refrigerator for another day.

3 Slice the mango in half through to the pit, then twist to remove the flesh from the pit. Peel and slice the flesh, set 4 slices aside and store the rest in the refrigerator for another day.

4 Mix the honey, orange and lemon rind, and ginger together in a bowl. Place the reserved pineapple, papaya, and mango on a grill rack with the kiwifruit, nectarines, and bananas. Brush the glaze over the fruit.

5 Cook the fruit under the preheated broiler for 10 minutes, brushing with the glaze and turning frequently. Divide between 4 serving plates and serve.

warm currants in cassis

serves 4   **prep: 10 mins**   **cook: 10 mins**

Crème de cassis is a black currant–based liqueur which comes from France and is an excellent flavoring for all types of fruit dishes. This dessert is the perfect way to end a meal, served with a little whipped cream or fat free mascarpone cheese.

INGREDIENTS

3 cups black currants

3 cups red currants

4 tbsp superfine sugar

grated rind and juice of 1 orange

2 tsp arrowroot

2 tbsp crème de cassis

whipped cream or fat free mascarpone cheese

4 fresh mint sprigs, to decorate

NUTRITIONAL INFORMATION	
Calories	.202
Protein	.2g
Carbohydrate	.35g
Sugars	.0g
Fat	.6g
Saturates	.4g

variation

Fresh berries would also work well. Use the same amount of fresh blackberries and strawberries.

cook's tip

When stripping the currants from their stalks, just run the tines of a fork down the length of the stalk and the currants will come away very easily.

1 Using a fork, strip the black currants and red currants from their stalks and place in a small, heavy-bottom pan.

2 Add the superfine sugar and orange rind and juice, and heat gently, stirring, until the sugar has dissolved. Bring to a boil and let simmer for 5 minutes.

3 Strain the currants through a strainer and place in a bowl, then return the juice to the pan. Blend the arrowroot with a little water and mix into the juice in the pan. Boil the mixture until thickened.

4 Remove the pan from the heat and let cool slightly, then stir in the crème de cassis. Transfer to 4 serving dishes, add a spoonful of whipped cream or mascarpone cheese and decorate with mint sprigs.

fig & watermelon salad

serves 4 | **prep: 15 mins,** ⏲ **plus 1 hr chilling** | **cook: 5 mins** ⏲

Fruit salads are always popular, and are quick and easy to prepare. Ring the changes with this attractive summery combination that looks almost too pretty to eat.

INGREDIENTS

1 watermelon, weighing about 3 lb 5 oz/1.5 kg

¾ cup seeded black grapes

4 figs

1 lime

grated rind and juice of 1 orange

1 tbsp maple syrup

2 tbsp honey

4 fresh mint sprigs, to decorate (optional)

NUTRITIONAL INFORMATION

Calories	169
Protein	2g
Carbohydrate	41g
Sugars	40g
Fat	1g
Saturates	0g

variation

Add 2 pieces of chopped preserved ginger to the fruit in Step 1 and replace 1 tablespoon of ginger syrup from the jar for the maple syrup.

1 Cut the watermelon into quarters and scoop out and discard the seeds. Cut the flesh away from the rind, then chop the flesh into 1-inch/2.5-cm cubes. Place the watermelon cubes in a bowl with the grapes. Cut each fig lengthwise into 8 wedges and add to the bowl.

2 Grate the lime rind and mix it with the orange rind and juice, maple syrup, and honey in a small pan. Bring to a boil over low heat. Pour the mixture over the fruit and stir. Let cool. Stir again, cover, and let chill in the refrigerator for at least 1 hour, stirring occasionally.

3 To serve, divide the fruit salad equally between 4 glass dishes and decorate with a fresh mint sprig, if you like.

stuffed baked apples

cook: 45 mins **prep: 10 mins** **serves 4**

Baked apples are a traditional family favorite, and are often stuffed with golden raisins, raisins, and brown sugar. Try this delicious ginger-flavored oat filling for a change.

NUTRITIONAL INFORMATION	
Calories	170
Protein	3g
Carbohydrate	31g
Sugars	23g
Fat	5g
Saturates	0g

INGREDIENTS

1 tbsp blanched almonds

⅓ cup no-soak dried apricots

1 piece preserved ginger, drained

1 tbsp honey

1 tbsp syrup from the preserved ginger jar

4 tbsp rolled oats

4 large cooking apples

 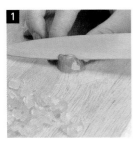 

variation

Use an extra tablespoon of honey instead of the ginger and syrup, replace the almonds with walnuts and add ½ teaspoon ground cinnamon.

1 Preheat the oven to 350°F/180°C. Using a sharp knife, chop the almonds very finely. Chop the apricots and preserved ginger very finely. Set aside.

2 Put the honey and syrup in a pan and heat until the honey has melted. Stir in the oats and cook gently over low heat for 2 minutes. Remove the pan from the heat and stir in the almonds, apricots, and preserved ginger.

3 Core the apples, widen the tops slightly and score round the circumference of each to prevent the skins from bursting during cooking. Place them in an ovenproof dish and fill the cavities with the filling. Pour just enough water into the dish to come about one-third of the way up the apples. Bake in the oven for 40 minutes, or until tender. Serve immediately.

hot chocolate cherries

serves 4   **prep: 15 mins** ⟲   **cook: 20–25 mins** ⏲

This is a naughty self-indulgence, but chocoholics don't have to forego their favorite fix and there is even heavy cream in this melt-in-the-mouth dessert. It makes a good finale to a dinner party.

INGREDIENTS

4 tbsp water

¼ cup superfine sugar

1 strip of pared lemon rind

1 lb/450 g sweet black cherries, pitted

1 tbsp unsweetened cocoa

pinch of salt

4 tbsp heavy cream

4 tbsp maraschino liqueur or cherry brandy

NUTRITIONAL INFORMATION

Calories 280

Protein 2g

Carbohydrate 31g

Sugars 31g

Fat 15g

Saturates 9g

variation

Instead of lemon rind, flavor the syrup with a vanilla bean and remove it in Step 2, or add ½ teaspoon vanilla extract with the liqueur in Step 3.

cook's tip

Don't substitute light cream for the heavy cream—even with the intention of lowering the fat content of this recipe—because it will curdle.

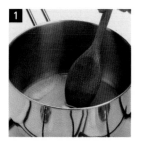

1 Preheat the broiler to medium. Put the water, sugar, and lemon rind in a pan and bring to a boil over low heat, stirring constantly, until the sugar has dissolved. Add the cherries and cook, stirring, for 1 minute. Remove from the heat. Using a slotted spoon, transfer the cherries to an ovenproof dish. Set aside the syrup.

2 Put the unsweetened cocoa in a bowl and mix in the salt. Whisking constantly, pour in the cream in a steady stream. Remove the lemon rind from the syrup and discard, then stir in the cream mixture. Return to the heat and bring to a boil, stirring. Let simmer the mixture over low heat for 10–15 minutes, or until reduced by about half.

3 Remove from the heat, and stir in the maraschino liqueur. Pour the sauce over the cherries. Cook under the preheated broiler for 2 minutes, then serve.

banana soufflés

serves 4   **prep: 10 mins**   **cook: 8 mins**

These elegant individual soufflés would be an excellent choice for a special dinner party dessert, especially as they are so simple to make. Like all soufflés, however, they must be served immediately, otherwise they will start to deflate.

INGREDIENTS

corn oil, for brushing

2 ripe bananas

1 tablespoon of lime juice

1 tablespoon of Malibu or other coconut liqueur

4 eggs, separated

generous ¼ cup superfine sugar

confectioners' sugar, for dusting

NUTRITIONAL INFORMATION

Calories 194
Protein 7g
Carbohydrate 27g
Sugars 26g
Fat 7g
Saturates 2g

variation

Replace the Malibu with ordinary rum or orange juice and substitute lemon juice for the lime juice.

cook's tip

To whisk egg whites well, make sure that they are as fresh as possible and that they are at room temperature. Use a clean, dry, greasefree bowl and a balloon whisk or electric beaters.

1 Preheat the oven to 450°F/230°C. Lightly brush 4 x 1½-cup/12-fl oz soufflé dishes with oil. Peel the bananas and cut into 1-inch/2.5-cm lengths, then place in a food processor with the lime juice and liqueur. Process until smooth. Add the egg yolks and 1 teaspoon of the sugar and process briefly again. Transfer to a bowl.

2 Place the egg whites in a spotlessly clean, greasefree bowl and whisk until stiff peaks form, then whisk in the remaining sugar, 1 tablespoon at a time, until the mixture becomes stiff and glossy. Fold 1 tablespoon of the egg white mixture into the banana mixture to loosen it, then gently incorporate the remainder.

3 Spoon the soufflé mixture into the prepared dishes and make a rim with the end of a teaspoon. Place on a baking sheet and bake in the preheated oven for 8 minutes, or until well risen and golden. Dust with confectioners' sugar and serve immediately.

nectarine crunch

serves 3   **prep: 10 mins** ⏲   **cook: 0 mins** ⏲

This incredibly easy and nutritious dessert is very popular with children, who even enjoy making it themselves. You can vary the fruit, fruit nectar, and jelly according to the season.

INGREDIENTS

4 nectarines

6 oz/175 g raisin and nut crunchy oat cereal

1¼ cups lowfat plain yogurt

2 tbsp peach jam

2 tbsp peach nectar

NUTRITIONAL INFORMATION

Calories 419

Protein 15g

Carbohydrate 83g

Sugars 52g

Fat 5g

Saturates 0g

cook's tip

There is no need to peel the nectarines—just wash and pat dry with paper towel. If you use peaches, they work better if they are peeled.

1 Using a sharp knife, cut the nectarines in half, then remove and discard the pits. Chop the flesh into bite-size pieces. Set aside a few pieces for decoration and place a few pieces in the bottom of 3 sundae glasses.

Place a layer of oat cereal in each glass, then drizzle over a little yogurt.

2 Place the jelly and peach nectar in a large pitcher and stir together to mix. Add a few more nectarine

pieces to the glasses and drizzle over a little of the jelly mixture. Continue building up the layers in this way, finishing with a layer of yogurt and a sprinkling of oat cereal. Decorate with the reserved nectarine pieces and serve.

lemon brûlées with red currants

cook: 10 mins **prep: 10 mins, plus 30 mins chilling** **serves 4**

Concealed beneath the caramelized topping is a surprising fruity sauce. Made with yogurt rather than cream, these little desserts are wonderful lowfat treats, which are perfect for any occasion.

NUTRITIONAL INFORMATION	
Calories	.250
Protein	.10g
Carbohydrate	.23g
Sugars	.23g
Fat	.14g
Saturates	.8g

INGREDIENTS

1 lemon

1½ cups red currants, plus extra
to decorate

3 tbsp superfine sugar

2 cups strained plain yogurt

¼ tsp ground cinnamon

1 Grate the rind from the lemon and set aside. Preheat the broiler to medium. Put the red currants and 1 tablespoon of the sugar in a small, heavy-bottom pan and cook over low heat until the juices start to run. Remove from the heat, stir in the lemon rind and set aside.

2 Mix the yogurt and ground cinnamon together in a bowl. Divide the red currants between 4 ramekins or small ovenproof dishes. Top with the cinnamon yogurt and sprinkle with the remaining sugar. Place under the preheated broiler for 4–5 minutes, or until the sugar is golden brown and bubbling.

Let cool, then let chill in the refrigerator for at least 30 minutes before serving. When ready to serve, decorate with the extra red currants.

variation

These brûlées are equally delicious made with other berries such as black currants, white currants, billberries, or blueberries.

berry yogurt ice

serves 4   **prep: 15 mins, ⏲ plus 4 hrs freezing**   **cook: 5 mins ⏲**

This refreshing ice makes a wonderful summer dessert after a filling meal, as it is light and cooling without the richness—or fat—of ice cream. Serve with a selection of fresh summer berries.

INGREDIENTS

generous 1 cup raspberries

generous 1 cup blackberries

generous 1 cup strawberries

1 large egg

¾ cup strained plain yogurt

½ cup red wine

2¼ tsp powdered gelatin

fresh berries, to decorate

NUTRITIONAL INFORMATION

Calories 118

Protein 6g

Carbohydrate 6g

Sugars 6g

Fat 6g

Saturates 3g

variation

Substitute ½ cup red currants for half the raspberries and ½ cup black currants for half the blackberries.

cook's tip

Vegetarians can use a vegetarian gelatin, which is available in health food stores, to make this ice. Follow the instructions on the package and proceed as in main recipe.

1 Put the raspberries, blackberries, and strawberries in a blender or food processor and process until a smooth purée forms. Press the purée through a strainer into a bowl to remove the seeds.

2 Break the egg and separate the yolk and white into separate bowls. Stir the egg yolk and yogurt into the berry purée and set the egg white aside.

3 Pour the wine into a heatproof bowl and sprinkle the gelatin on the surface. Let stand for 5 minutes to soften, then set the bowl over a pan of simmering water until the gelatin has dissolved. Pour the mixture into the berry purée in a steady stream, whisking constantly. Transfer the mixture to a freezerproof container and freeze for 2 hours, or until slushy.

4 Whisk the egg white in a spotlessly clean, greasefree bowl until very stiff. Remove the berry mixture from the freezer and fold in the egg white. Return to the freezer and freeze for 2 hours, or until firm. To serve, scoop the berry yogurt ice into glass dishes and decorate with fresh berries of your choice.

coffee ice cream

serves 6   **prep: 1 hr, plus 6 hrs freezing**   **cook: 0 mins**

This Italian-style dessert tastes as if it is full of heavy cream. In fact, it isn't an ice cream at all. If you have an espresso machine, make the coffee in that, otherwise brew it double strength in a filter.

INGREDIENTS

1 square semisweet chocolate

1 cup ricotta cheese

5 tbsp lowfat plain yogurt

⅜ cup superfine sugar

¾ cup strong black coffee, cooled and chilled

½ tsp ground cinnamon

dash of vanilla extract

generous 2 tbsp chocolate curls, to decorate

NUTRITIONAL INFORMATION	
Calories	150
Protein	.6g
Carbohydrate	21g
Sugars	21g
Fat	.6g
Saturates	.4g

variation

Omit the cinnamon and vanilla extract and substitute 1½ squares grated mint chocolate for the semisweet chocolate.

1 Grate the chocolate and set aside. Put the ricotta cheese, yogurt, and sugar in a blender or food processor and process until a smooth purée forms. Transfer to a large bowl and beat in the coffee, cinnamon, vanilla extract, and grated chocolate.

2 Spoon the mixture into a freezerproof container

and freeze for 1½ hours, or until slushy. Remove from the freezer, turn into a bowl, and beat. Return to the container and freeze for 1½ hours.

3 Repeat this beating and freezing process twice more before serving in scoops, decorated with chocolate curls. Alternatively, leave in the freezer until 15 minutes before

serving, then transfer to the refrigerator to soften slightly before scooping.

lemon granita

⏲ **cook: 5 mins**   🕐 **prep: 10 mins,**   **serves 4**
                          plus 2 hrs freezing

Not quite a sherbet, but more than a cold drink, a granita is a deliciously refreshing way to cleanse the palate, and is an ideal dessert to serve after a spicy main course.

NUTRITIONAL INFORMATION	
Calories	.115
Protein	.0g
Carbohydrate	.31g
Sugars	.31g
Fat	.0g
Saturates	.0g

INGREDIENTS

2 cups water

½ cup sugar

grated rind of 1 lemon

8 tbsp freshly squeezed lemon juice

lemon zest, to decorate

variation

You can substitute the grated rind of ½ orange and the same quantity of orange juice for the lemon rind and juice, if you like.

1 Put the water and sugar in a large, heavy-bottom pan and set over low heat. Stir constantly until the sugar has completely dissolved. Bring to a boil, then remove the pan from the heat and let cool.

2 Add the lemon rind and juice to the cooled syrup and stir well to combine, then pour the mixture into a large, shallow, freezerproof container and freeze for 2 hours, or until the lemon syrup is solid.

3 Plunge the bottom of the container into hot water for 30 seconds, then turn out the frozen syrup into a food processor. Process to small crystals, then spoon into serving bowls, and decorate with lemon zest. Serve immediately.

peach sherbet

serves 4

prep: 10 mins, ⟳
plus 2 hrs freezing

cook: 0 mins ⟳

This is a cheating, but still effective way of making a luscious frozen dessert, full of intense fruit flavor. Serve in small dessert bowls as part of a dinner party menu.

INGREDIENTS

3 large, ripe peaches

1 tbsp lemon juice

1 tbsp honey

1 tsp Southern Comfort or peach schnapps

peach leaves, to decorate

NUTRITIONAL INFORMATION

Calories 57

Protein 1g

Carbohydrate 13g

Sugars 13g

Fat 0g

Saturates 0g

variation

For a virtually instant strawberry sherbet, buy 1 lb 2 oz/500 g frozen strawberries and process as in main recipe with honey and Curaçao.

cook's tip

To peel a whole peach, make a tiny nick in the skin and place in a bowl. Cover with boiling water and leave for 15 seconds. Remove using a slotted spoon. Peel off the skin.

1 Using a sharp knife, cut the peaches in half, then remove and discard the pits. Place the peach halves in a bowl of boiling water and let stand for 15 seconds. Remove from the bowl using a slotted spoon and peel off the skins. Cut the peaches into 1-inch/2.5-cm chunks and toss with the lemon juice. Spread the chunks out on a baking sheet, cover and freeze for 2 hours, or until solid.

2 Remove the peaches from the freezer and place in a food processor. Pulse until granular, scraping down the sides from time to time.

3 Add the honey and Southern Comfort and process again until thoroughly blended and fairly firm in consistency. Serve immediately, decorated with peach leaves or place in a freezerproof container and store in the freezer for up to 24 hours.

citrus meringue crush

⏱ **cook: 10 mins**

🕐 **prep: 1 hr,
plus 2 hrs freezing**

serves 4

NUTRITIONAL INFORMATION

Calories	.165
Protein	.5g
Carbohydrate	.37g
Sugars	.32g
Fat	.1g
Saturates	.0.4g

variation

You can replace the orange liqueur with the same amount of unsweetened orange juice, if you like.

This is an excellent way to use up any leftover meringue shells and is easy and simple to prepare. Serve immediately with a spoonful of tangy kumquat sauce.

INGREDIENTS

8 ready-made meringue nests

1¼ cups lowfat plain yogurt

½ tsp finely grated orange rind

½ tsp finely grated lemon rind

½ tsp finely grated lime rind

2 tbsp orange liqueur

2 tbsp lime juice

2 tbsp water

2–3 tsp superfine sugar

1 tsp cornstarch mixed
with 1 tbsp water

SAUCE

2 oz/55 g kumquats

8 tbsp unsweetened orange juice

TO DECORATE

sliced kumquat

strips of lime rind

cook's tip

Kumquats are available from most large supermarkets. When buying, always choose ones that are unblemished. Before using, wash thoroughly under cold running water.

1 Place the meringues in a plastic bag and using a rolling pin, crush into small pieces. Place in a bowl. Stir in the yogurt, grated citrus rinds, and the liqueur. Spoon the mixture into 4 mini-bowls and freeze for 1½–2 hours, or until firm.

2 To make the sauce, using a sharp knife, thinly slice the kumquats and place them in a small pan with the fruit juices and water. Bring to a boil and let simmer over low heat for 3–4 minutes, or until the kumquats soften.

3 Sweeten with sugar to taste, stir in the cornstarch mixture and cook, stirring, until thickened. Pour into a small bowl, cover the surface with plastic wrap and let cool—the film will help prevent a skin forming. Let chill in the refrigerator until required.

4 To serve, dip the meringue bowls in hot water for 5 seconds, or until they loosen, then turn them out onto 4 serving plates. Spoon over a little sauce, decorate with slices of kumquat, and strips of lime rind and serve immediately.

chocolate cheese pots

serves 4　　　**prep: 10 mins, plus** ⏲ **30 mins chilling**　　　**cook: 0 mins** ⏲

These super-light desserts are just the thing if you have a craving for chocolate. They are delicious served on their own or with a selection of fresh fruit.

INGREDIENTS

1¼ cups fat free mascarpone cheese

⅔ cup lowfat plain yogurt

¼ cup confectioners' sugar

4 tsp lowfat drinking chocolate powder

4 tsp unsweetened cocoa

1 tsp vanilla extract

2 tbsp dark rum (optional)

2 medium egg whites

4 chocolate shapes, to decorate

TO SERVE

pieces of kiwifruit, orange, and banana

whole strawberries and raspberries

NUTRITIONAL INFORMATION

Calories	177
Protein	. . . . .9g
Carbohydrate	. . . . .18g
Sugars	. . . . .17g
Fat	. . . . .1g
Saturates	. . . . .1g

variation

If liked, arrange ¾ cup mixed summer berries in the bases before adding the mousse.

cook's tip

This mixture would make a good cheesecake filling. Make the base from crushed amaretti cookies and egg white and set the filling with 2 teaspoons powdered gelatin dissolved in 2 tablespoons boiling water.

1 Mix the mascarpone cheese and yogurt together in a bowl. Sift in the sugar, chocolate, and cocoa and mix well. Add the vanilla extract and rum, if using.

2 Whisk the egg whites in a separate spotlessly clean, greasefree bowl until stiff. Using a metal spoon, gently fold the egg whites into the chocolate mixture.

3 Spoon the mascarpone cheese and chocolate mixture into 4 small china dessert pots or ramekins and let chill in the refrigerator for 30 minutes.

4 Decorate each chocolate cheese pot with a chocolate shape and serve with an assortment of fresh fruit, such as pieces of kiwifruit, orange, and banana, and a few whole strawberries and raspberries.

indonesian black rice pudding

serves 4 **prep: 5 mins** ⏲ **cook: 45 mins** ⏲

Also known as glutinous rice, even though it doesn't contain any gluten, sticky rice is available from Chinese supermarkets and may be black or white—the former is unpolished.

INGREDIENTS

½ cup black sticky rice

2 cups water

¼ cup dark brown sugar

¼ cup superfine sugar

1¼ cups coconut milk, to serve

NUTRITIONAL INFORMATION

Calories 228

Protein 3g

Carbohydrate 54g

Sugars 33g

Fat 1g

Saturates 0g

variation

Add a small piece of bruised fresh gingerroot when cooking the rice to add extra flavor. Remove and discard before serving.

1 Rinse the black sticky rice under cold running water, drain and place in a large, heavy-bottom pan. Add the water and bring to a boil, stirring constantly. Cover and let simmer over medium–low heat for 30 minutes.

2 Stir in the sugars and cook for an additional 15 minutes. If necessary, add a little more water to prevent the rice from sticking.

3 Ladle the rice into 4 warmed bowls and serve immediately with the coconut milk. Alternatively, let cool completely and serve cold.

magic cheesecake

⏲ **cook: 5 mins**　　　　　🕒 **prep: 15 mins,**　　　　　**serves 6**
　　　　　　　　　　　　　　　plus 1 hr chilling

This superb dessert proves that you can have your cake and eat it too—or rather, you can indulge in a wonderful creamy and luxurious cheesecake and still stick to a healthy lowfat diet.

NUTRITIONAL INFORMATION	
Calories 175	
Protein 9g	
Carbohydrate 22g	
Sugars 12g	
Fat 6g	
Saturates 2g	

INGREDIENTS

12 oz/350 g mixed fruits, such as carambola, kiwifruit, strawberries, and kumquats

4 oz/115 g bran flakes, crushed

½ cup lowfat spread

10 oz/280 g firm tofu (drained weight)

generous ¾ cup lowfat plain yogurt

1 tbsp powdered gelatin

6 tbsp apple juice

variation

If you like, try adding some finely grated lemon rind and the juice of 1 lemon to the yogurt and tofu mixture for extra flavor.

1 Prepare the fruits to lay on top of the cheesecake by washing, seeding, peeling, and slicing, as necessary, and set aside. Place the bran flakes in a plastic bag and crush them with a rolling pin.

2 Place the lowfat spread and 2 tablespoons of the apple juice in a pan over very low heat and stir. When the spread has melted, stir in the bran flakes. Turn the mixture into a 9-inch/23-cm loose-bottom cake pan and press down with a spoon to cover the bottom. Set aside.

3 Put the tofu and yogurt in a food processor and process until smooth, then transfer to a bowl. Pour the remaining apple juice into a heatproof bowl, sprinkle the gelatin over the surface and let stand for 5 minutes to soften. Set the bowl over a pan of simmering water for 5 minutes, or until the gelatin has dissolved, then pour into the tofu mixture in a steady stream, beating constantly. Spread over the bottom and let chill until set.

4 Remove the cheesecake from the pan and place on a serving plate. Arrange the mixed fruits on top and serve.

almond cheesecakes

⏲ **cook: 10 mins**

🕐 **prep: 15 mins,**
plus 1 hr chilling

serves 4

NUTRITIONAL INFORMATION

Calories 361

Protein 16g

Carbohydrate 43g

Sugars 29g

Fat 15g

Saturates 4g

variation

Instead of the amaretti cookies for the base, use crushed gingersnaps. You can also substitute lemon for the lime.

These creamy cheese desserts are so delicious that it's hard to believe that they are low in fat. Served with plenty of fresh fruit, such as strawberries, blackberries, and peaches, they are excellent for all special occasions.

INGREDIENTS

12 amaretti cookies

1 medium egg white, lightly beaten

1 cup skim milk soft cheese

½ tsp almond extract

½ tsp finely grated lime rind

generous ¼ cup ground almonds

2 tbsp superfine sugar

⅓ cup golden raisins

2 tsp powdered gelatin

2 tbsp boiling water

2 tbsp lime juice

TO DECORATE

¼ cup toasted slivered almonds

strips of lime rind

cook's tip

When using parchment paper, it is not necessary to oil the paper beforehand as the food very easily peels off after baking.

1 Preheat the oven to 350°F/180°C. Place the cookies in a large, clean plastic bag, seal the bag and using a rolling pin, crush them into small pieces.

2 Place the crumbs in a large bowl and bind together with the egg white.

3 Arrange 4 nonstick pastry rings or poached egg rings, 3½ inches/9 cm across, on a baking sheet lined with parchment paper. Divide the cookie mixture into 4 equal portions and spoon it into the rings, pressing down well. Bake in the preheated oven for 10 minutes, or until crisp. Let cool in the rings.

4 Beat the soft cheese, almond extract, lime rind, ground almonds, sugar, and golden raisins together until well mixed. Dissolve the gelatin in the boiling water and stir in the lime juice. Fold into the cheese mixture and spoon over the cookie bases. Smooth the tops and let chill in the refrigerator for 1 hour, or until

set. Loosen the cheesecakes from the rings using a small spatula and transfer to serving plates. Decorate with toasted slivered almonds and strips of lime rind and serve.

brown sugar pavlovas

serves 4 **prep: 25 mins, plus 1 hr cooling** **cook: 1 hr**

This simple combination of fudgy meringue topped with fat free mascarpone cheese and raspberries is the perfect end to any meal.

INGREDIENTS

2 large egg whites

1 tsp cornstarch

1 tsp raspberry vinegar

½ cup firmly packed light brown sugar, crushed free of lumps

2 tbsp red currant jelly

2 tbsp unsweetened orange juice

⅔ cup fat free mascarpone cheese

⅔ cup raspberries, thawed if frozen

rose-scented geranium leaves, to decorate (optional)

NUTRITIONAL INFORMATION

Calories	155
Protein	51g
Carbohydrate	35g
Sugars	34g
Fat	0.4g
Saturates	2g

cook's tip

Make a large pavlova by forming the meringue into a circle, measuring 7 inches/ 18 cm across, on a lined baking sheet and bake in the preheated oven for 1 hour.

1 Preheat the oven to 300°F/150°C. Line a large baking sheet with parchment paper. Whisk the egg whites in a spotlessly clean, greasefree bowl until very stiff and dry. Fold in the cornstarch and vinegar. Gradually whisk in the sugar, a spoonful at a time, until the mixture is thick and glossy.

2 Divide the mixture into 4 portions and spoon onto the prepared baking sheet, spaced well apart. Smooth each portion into a circle, 4 inches/10 cm across, and bake in the preheated oven for 40–45 minutes, or until lightly browned and crisp. Let cool on the baking sheet until cold.

3 Place the red currant jelly and orange juice in a small pan and heat, stirring constantly, until melted. Remove the pan from the heat and let cool for 10 minutes. Using a spatula, carefully remove each pavlova from the parchment paper and transfer to a serving plate. Top with the mascarpone cheese and the raspberries. Glaze the fruit with the red currant jelly and decorate with the geranium leaves, if using.

paper-thin fruit pies

 cook: 15–20 mins   prep: 20 mins   serves 4

*The extra-crisp pastry shells, filled with slices of fruit and glazed
with apricot jelly, are best served hot with lowfat custard.*

NUTRITIONAL INFORMATION

Calories	158
Protein	2g
Carbohydrate	14g
Sugars	0g
Fat	10g
Saturates	1g

INGREDIENTS

1 medium eating apple

1 medium ripe pear

2 tbsp lemon juice

4 tbsp lowfat spread

4 rectangular sheets of phyllo pastry,
thawed if frozen

2 tbsp low sugar apricot jelly

1 tbsp unsweetened orange juice

1 tbsp finely chopped natural pistachio
nuts, shelled

2 tsp confectioners' sugar, for dusting

lowfat custard, to serve

cook's tip

Other combinations of fresh
fruit are equally delicious.
Try peach and apricot,
raspberry and apple,
or mango and pineapple.

1 Preheat the oven to 400°F/200°C. Core and thinly slice the apple and pear and toss them in the lemon juice. Gently melt the lowfat spread over low heat.

2 Cut the sheets of pastry into 4 and cover with a clean, damp dish towel. Brush 4 nonstick shallow baking dishes, measuring 4 inch/ 10 cm across, with a little of the lowfat spread.

3 Working on each pie separately, brush 4 sheets of pastry with lowfat spread. Press a small sheet of pastry into the bottom of one dish. Arrange the other sheets of pastry on top at slightly different angles. Repeat with the other sheets of pastry to make another 3 pies.

4 Arrange the apple and pear slices alternately in the center of each pastry shell and lightly crimp the edges of the pastry of each pie. Mix the jelly and orange juice together until smooth, then brush over the fruit. Bake in the preheated oven for 12–15 minutes. Sprinkle with pistachio nuts, dust lightly with confectioners' sugar and serve with custard.

carrot & ginger cake

cook: 1 hr 15 mins

prep: 15 mins, plus 1 hr 20 mins cooling

serves 10

NUTRITIONAL INFORMATION

Calories 249

Protein 7g

Carbohydrate 46g

Sugars 28g

Fat 6g

Saturates 1g

variation

Instead of the topping, sprinkle a few pine nuts and crushed sugar lumps on top of the cake before baking.

This melt-in-the-mouth version of a favorite cake has a fraction of the fat of the traditional cake.

INGREDIENTS

butter, for greasing

scant 1 cup all-purpose flour

1 tsp baking powder

1 tsp baking soda

2 tsp ground ginger

½ tsp salt

scant ⅞ cup light brown sugar

8 oz/225 g carrots, grated

2 pieces preserved ginger in syrup, drained and chopped

1 oz/25 g fresh gingerroot, grated

⅓ cup seedless raisins

2 medium eggs, beaten

3 tbsp corn oil

juice of 1 medium orange

FROSTING

1 cup lowfat soft cheese

4 tbsp confectioners' sugar

1 tsp vanilla extract

TO DECORATE

preserved ginger pieces

freshly grated gingerroot

cook's tip

If you have a grater attachment on your food processor this will speed up the grating of the carrots. Remember to peel the carrots first.

1 Preheat the oven to 350°F/180°C. Grease and line an 8-inch/20-cm round cake pan with parchment paper.

2 Sift the flour, baking powder, baking soda, ground ginger, and salt into a bowl. Stir in the sugar, carrots, preserved ginger, gingerroot, and raisins. Beat the eggs,

corn oil, and orange juice together, then pour into the bowl. Mix well.

3 Spoon the mixture into the prepared pan and bake in the preheated oven for 1–1¼ hours, or until firm to the touch and a tip of a knife inserted into the center of the cake comes out clean. Let cool in the pan.

4 To make the frosting, place the soft cheese in a bowl and beat to soften. Sift in the confectioners' sugar and add the vanilla extract. Mix well. Remove the cake from the pan and smooth the frosting over the top. Decorate the cake with pieces of preserved ginger and a little grated fresh ginger, then serve.

apricot cake

serves 8 **prep: 20 mins, plus** ⏲ **40 mins cooling/chilling** **cook: 1 hr 15 mins** ⏲

The moist, fruity layer of filling makes this lovely light cake a welcome treat with a cup of mid-morning coffee or as a dessert at the end of a midweek family supper.

INGREDIENTS

BASE

scant 1½ cups plain flour, plus

extra for dusting

pinch of salt

¼ cup superfine sugar

grated rind of ½ lemon

4 tbsp water

6 tbsp unsalted butter, softened

FILLING

generous ½ cup short-grain rice

2 cups skim milk

scant ⅓ cup superfine sugar

grated rind and juice of ½ lemon

1 tbsp apricot jelly

3 eggs, separated

1 lb 12 oz/800 g apricots, peeled, halved, and pitted

confectioners' sugar, for dusting

NUTRITIONAL INFORMATION

Calories	377
Protein	9g
Carbohydrate	63g
Sugars	24g
Fat	12g
Saturates	7g

variation

For a change, replace the grated lemon rind and juice in the base and filling with the same amount of grated orange rind and juice.

cook's tip

To bake blind, prick the base all over with a fork, then line with parchment paper. Partially fill with dried beans—either ceramic pie weights, rice, or dried beans kept specially for the purpose—and bake.

1 Preheat the oven to 400°F/200°C. Sift the flour with a pinch of salt into a bowl and add the sugar, lemon rind, water, and butter. Mix well, using an electric mixer or fork, until crumbly. Turn out onto a lightly floured counter and knead lightly until smooth. Roll out and use to line the bottom and 1¼-inches/3-cm of the sides of

a 10-inch/25-cm springform cake pan. Let chill in the refrigerator for 30 minutes, then bake blind in the oven for 10 minutes (see Cook's Tip).

2 Meanwhile, make the filling. Put the rice, milk, sugar, and lemon rind in a small, heavy-bottom pan and bring to a boil. Reduce the heat and let simmer for

30 minutes. Remove the pan from the heat, stir in the lemon juice and apricot jelly and let cool.

3 Stir the egg yolks into the cooled rice mixture. Whisk the egg whites in a clean bowl until stiff, then fold gently into the rice mixture. Remove the cooked base from the oven, discard the dried

beans and lining paper and reduce the oven temperature to 350°F/180°C. Arrange the apricot halves, flat side uppermost, over the base. Spoon the rice mixture over the top, spreading it out evenly. Bake for 45 minutes, or until the tip of a knife inserted into the cake comes out clean. Cool and dust with confectioners' sugar before serving.

strawberry roulade

serves 8 **prep: 30 mins, plus** 🕒 **30 mins cooling** **cook: 10 mins** 🕒

Serve this moist, light sponge rolled up with a tasty almond and strawberry mascarpone cheese filling for a delicious teatime treat.

INGREDIENTS

3 large eggs

scant ⅔ cup superfine sugar

scant ⅞ cup all-purpose flour

1 tbsp hot water

FILLING

scant 1 cup lowfat mascarpone cheese

1 tsp almond extract

scant ⅞ cup small strawberries

⅛ cup slivered almonds, toasted

1 tsp confectioners' sugar

NUTRITIONAL INFORMATION	
Calories 166	
Protein 6g	
Carbohydrate 30g	
Sugars 19g	
Fat 3g	
Saturates 1g	

variation

Replace the strawberries with other fresh fruit, such as mixed summer berries, a mix of red and green grapes, or banana and kiwifruit slices.

cook's tip

To prevent the sponge from breaking when you roll it up with the filling in place, manipulate it with the parchment paper not your fingers, and work slowly and carefully.

1 Preheat the oven to 425°F/220°C. Line a 14 x 10-inch/35 x 25-cm jelly roll pan with parchment paper. Place the eggs in a large bowl with the superfine sugar, place over a pan of hot water and, using an electric whisk, whisk until pale and thick.

2 Remove the bowl from the pan. Sift in the

flour and fold into the eggs with the hot water. Pour the mixture into the prepared pan and bake in the preheated oven for 8–10 minutes, or until golden and set.

3 Transfer the sponge to a sheet of parchment paper. Carefully peel off the lining paper and roll up the sponge tightly, along with the

parchment paper. Wrap the sponge in a dish towel and let cool until cold.

4 Mix the mascarpone cheese and almond extract together in a bowl. Set aside a few strawberries for the decoration, wash, hull, and slice the rest. Let the mixture chill in the refrigerator until required.

5 Unroll the sponge, spread the mascarpone cheese mixture over the sponge and sprinkle with strawberries. Roll the sponge up again and transfer to a serving plate. Sprinkle with almonds and lightly dust with confectioners' sugar. Decorate with the reserved strawberries and serve.

fat free marble cake

serves 8   **prep: 25 mins, plus** ⟲ **30 mins cooling**   **cook: 45 mins** ⏲

For those of us who have a particularly sweet tooth, this beautifully light cake is too good to be true. The secret of its success lies in sifting the flour several times.

INGREDIENTS

corn oil, for brushing

generous ¾ cup all-purpose flour, sifted, plus extra for dusting

3 tbsp unsweetened cocoa

generous 1 cup superfine sugar

pinch of salt

10 egg whites

1 tsp cream of tartar

½ tsp almond extract

½ tsp vanilla extract

confectioners' sugar, for dusting

NUTRITIONAL INFORMATION

Calories	186
Protein	6g
Carbohydrate	40g
Sugars	30g
Fat	1g
Saturates	1g

cook's tip

When removing the baked cake from the oven, leave inverted in the pan on a wire rack, then tap the bottom gently all the way round. This will release it from the pan.

1 Preheat the oven to 350°F/180°C. Oil and dust an 8-inch/20-cm deep cake pan. Sift ⅓ cup of the flour with the unsweetened cocoa and 2 tablespoons of the sugar into a bowl 4 times. Sift the remaining flour with 2 tablespoons of the sugar and the salt into a separate bowl 4 times.

2 Beat the egg whites in a spotlessly clean, greasefree bowl until soft peaks form. Add the cream of tartar and beat in the remaining superfine sugar, 1 tablespoonful at a time, until the egg whites form stiff peaks. Whisk in the almond and vanilla extracts. Divide the mixture in half. Fold the cocoa and flour mixture into one half and the unflavored flour into the other half. Spoon the cocoa flavored mixture into the pan and top with the unflavored mixture. Run a round-bladed knife through both mixtures to create a marbled effect.

3 Bake in the preheated oven for 45 minutes, or until the tip of a knife inserted into the center of the cake comes out clean. Invert onto a wire rack to cool and dust with confectioners' sugar before serving.

citrus honey cake

⏲ **cook: 35 mins**   ⏱ **prep: 20 mins, plus 30 mins cooling**   **serves 8**

This light-textured cake is drizzled with honey and lemon juice while it is still warm from the oven, giving it a rich and zesty flavor. Serve as a delicious dessert or a tasty afternoon snack.

NUTRITIONAL INFORMATION	
Calories	158
Protein	4g
Carbohydrate	30g
Sugars	11g
Fat	3g
Saturates	1g

INGREDIENTS

sunflower oil, for brushing

generous ¼ cup reduced fat sunflower margarine

4 tbsp honey

finely grated rind and juice of 1 lemon

⅔ cup skim milk

1 cup all-purpose flour

1½ tsp baking powder

½ teaspoon allspice

⅓ cup semolina

2 egg whites

2 tsp sesame seeds

cook's tip

Greek Hymettus honey, which has a distinctive aroma of thyme, would be especially delicious in this cake, as would the less expensive lemon blossom honey.

1 Preheat the oven to 400°F/200°C. Lightly brush a 9-inch/23-cm round cake pan with oil and line the bottom with parchment paper. Put the margarine and 3 tablespoons of the honey in a heavy-bottom pan and melt over very low heat. Remove from the heat. Set aside 1 tablespoon of the lemon juice and stir the remainder into the honey mixture with the lemon rind and milk.

2 Sift the flour, baking powder, and allspice into a bowl, then beat the mixture into the pan. Beat in the semolina. Whisk the egg whites in a separate spotlessly clean, greasefree bowl until soft peaks form, then gently fold them into the mixture.

Spoon into the prepared pan and smooth the surface. Sprinkle the sesame seeds evenly on top.

3 Bake the cake in the preheated oven for 30 minutes, or until golden brown and springy to the touch. Mix the remaining honey and lemon juice in a small pitcher and pour it over the cake. Let cool in the pan before serving.

fruit loaf with apple spread

serves 4   **prep: 15 mins, plus ⟳ 1 hr soaking/cooling**   **cook: 2 hrs ⟳**

This sweet, fruity loaf is ideal served for teatime or as a healthy snack at any time of the day. The fruit spread can be made quickly while the cake is baking in the oven.

INGREDIENTS

corn oil, for brushing

2 cups rolled oats

½ cup firmly packed light brown sugar

1 tsp ground cinnamon

¾ cup golden raisins

1 cup seedless raisins

2 tbsp malt extract

1¼ cups unsweetened apple juice

1 cup self-rising whole-wheat flour

1½ tsp baking powder

SPREAD

scant ⅛ cup strawberries, washed and hulled

2 eating apples, cored and chopped

1¼ cups unsweetened apple juice

TO SERVE

whole strawberries

apple wedges

NUTRITIONAL INFORMATION	
Calories	733
Protein	12g
Carbohydrate	17g
Sugars	110g
Fat	5g
Saturates	1g

variation

For a change, replace the strawberries with apple and blackberries or even strawberries and blackberries.

cook's tip

After preparing apples, sprinkle 1 tablespoon of lemon juice over them and mix until the apple pieces are coated as this prevents them discoloring.

1 Preheat the oven to 350°F/180°C. Oil and line a 2-lb/900-g loaf pan with parchment paper.

2 Place the rolled oats, sugar, cinnamon, golden raisins, raisins, and malt extract in a bowl. Pour in the apple juice, stir well and let soak for 30 minutes.

3 Sift in the flour and baking powder, adding any husks that remain in the strainer and fold in using a metal spoon.

4 Spoon the mixture into the prepared pan and bake in the preheated oven for 1½ hours, or until firm and a tip of a knife inserted into the

center comes out clean. Let cool in the pan for 10 minutes, then turn out onto a wire rack and let cool.

5 Meanwhile, make the fruit spread. Place the strawberries and apples in a pan and pour in the apple juice. Bring to a boil, cover, and let simmer for 30 minutes.

Beat the sauce well and spoon into a clean, warmed jar. Let cool, then seal and label. Serve the loaf with 1–2 tablespoons of the spread and strawberries and apple wedges.